Internet-Based Student Research

Creating to Learn with a Step-by-Step Approach, Grades 5–12

Twin Peaks Middle School

Internet-Based Student Research

Creating to Learn with a Step-by-Step Approach, Grades 5–12

By Jacqueline P. Keane

Edited by Carmen M. Walsh

Linworth Publishing, Inc.

Library of Congress Cataloging-in-Publication Data

Keane, Jacqueline P.
  Internet-based student research : creating to learn with a step-by-step approach, grades 5-12 / by Jacqueline P.
      Keane ; edited by Carmen M. Walsh.
      p. cm.
  Includes bibliographical references and index.
   ISBN 1-58683-209-3 (pbk.)
   1. Teaching—Computer network resources. 2. Computer-assisted instruction. 3. Internet in education. 4.
Research—Study and teaching. I. Walsh, Carmen M. II. Title.
LB1044.87K42 2006
371.33'4678—dc22
                              2006007054

Author: Jacqueline P. Keane

Linworth Books:
Carol Simpson, Editorial Director
Judi Repman, Associate Editor

Published by Linworth Publishing, Inc.
480 East Wilson Bridge Road, Suite L
Worthington, Ohio 43085

ISBN: 1-58683-209-3

5 4 3 2 1

To my husband, Dave —

*Thank you for working with me to get my thoughts on paper
and for inspiring me to write down my ideas.*

Thank you for all the confidence you have in me.

Table of Contents

Student Handouts

Preface

Internet-Based Student Research: Creating to Learn with a Step-by-Step Approach is an outgrowth of the last seven years of my life as an educator. Some of those years were spent teaching in my own classroom, and some were spent working as a consultant, assisting teachers of all grade levels. This book addresses needs that my students and I identified, as well as other topics I've discussed with teachers, consultants, and administrators.

I wrote this book to inspire teachers to examine their present teaching methodologies and to challenge them to seek better ways of infusing instructional technology into their classrooms. It offers a new approach to teaching and learning that intertwines effective established teaching practices with the instructional technology that is already available in most schools.

The time has come for a teaching methodology that requires students to become innovative, self-reliant, creative, and productive. *Internet-Based Student Research: Creating to Learn with a Step-by-Step Approach* offers teachers and administrators a new and structured approach to project-based learning that covers required content standards, infuses instructional technology, and prepares students for state testing and for "real-world" activities while advancing their own individuality, creativity, and uniqueness.

Students thrive in the active learning environment that is created when the theories and philosophies presented in this book are implemented. Class time is focused on presenting students with intellectually stimulating questions and on encouraging them to construct their own answers to these questions. Students are then challenged to develop and create unique demonstrations of their understandings and opinions. The methodology in this book not only places students at the center of the learning environment, but also focuses on exploring their understanding of the subject matter while at the same time probing, defining, developing, and actualizing their individuality.

Internet-Based Student Research: Creating to Learn with a Step-by-Step Approach helps teachers explain to students in grades 5–12 how to use an active learning model when working on their projects. It demonstrates best practices for using instructional technology, providing clear step-by-step directions, to enrich students' projects—and learning—with the technology available to most educators today.

— Jacqueline Keane

About the Author

A classroom teacher, instructional technology facilitator, researcher, and writer, Jacqueline P. Keane has won respect and awards for her excellence and innovation. As a valued member of Ramapo Central School District's instructional technology team, she has been active in visiting and studying the instructional technology integration models of some of the most acclaimed districts in New York and throughout the country. She has also visited Georgia, Texas, California, and Louisiana to examine the instructional technology models being implemented in their schools.

Jackie started her career in education as a social studies/language arts teacher at Wareham Middle School in Massachusetts. Building on her experience as a classroom teacher, she then became an instructional technology facilitator for the Ramapo Central School District. In that position, she has had the opportunity to consult and collaborate with teachers across all disciplines and grade levels to design technology-rich curriculum units within her Creating to Learn framework (www.KeaneIdeasInc.com). These units employ instructional technology in an approach that advances students' information literacy, visual literacy, and technical literacy skills. Jackie has analyzed and collected quantitative data from students and staff regarding the strengths and weaknesses of her approach to these skills. Based on this data and extensive fieldwork, she has improved her processes and has had the opportunity to share her final work with building and district administrators as well as outside educational consultants.

After graduating from Sayville High School in Long Island, New York, Jackie pursued her studies at Providence College, where she majored in history and secondary education. She completed her Master of Education at Framingham State College with a concentration in curriculum development and instructional technology. Jackie recently finished a Certificate of Advanced Graduate Study at SUNY New Paltz with a concentration in educational leadership and administration.

About the Editor

Carmen M. Walsh is a writer, editor, and publication designer with intensive experience in education and health care. She brings to her projects a clear, audience-friendly writing style—effective whether the audience is a pharmaceutical company's executive management or a classroom of teenage students.

Through her business, Walsh Writing (www.walshwriting.com), Carmen works with a variety of clients, including pharmaceutical manufacturers, marketing research organizations, educational companies, and literary publishers. She helps her clients create and improve their written materials, including books, reports, newsletters, brochures, profiles, Web content, and PowerPoint presentations.

Carmen graduated summa cum laude from Towson University with a master's degree in professional writing. She has also served as an adjunct writing instructor at the university.

Acknowledgments

As you read through *Internet-Based Student Research: Creating to Learn with a Step-by-Step Approach*, you can see many of the exchanges that have influenced my writing and my creation of new ideas. I am grateful for all the efforts of students, teachers, administrators, and education professionals who assisted and challenged me.

In particular, I would like to thank my editor, Carmen Walsh, who worked long, hard hours to help me craft my manuscript into a smooth and attractive book design. Over the last two years, Carmen has lent her talent and editorial expertise to the project, and I am proud to say she has also become a friend, always offering words of encouragement and support.

I am extremely grateful to Ricky Swain, who at the last minute provided us with illustrations for the book. His artistic creativity was a perfect match for the theme and design of this book.

I am also grateful to my husband, Dave, who spent hours working with me on the manuscript. His ideas, questions, and insights helped me to further clarify my own thoughts on the subject material.

Special thanks also to Jamie McKenzie, who has been an invaluable mentor; his encouragement and enthusiasm have been a valued source of motivation. I would also like to thank my colleagues, including Patricia Carney, Eleanor Cerny, Jenn Chiaravalle, Angelique Edwards, Melani Hampel, and Kathy Higgins for such stimulating collegial conversations about instructional technology. Furthermore, I would like to thank John Collins for working with me and being my first guinea pig in field-testing the CIDE process.

I give special thanks to Marlene Woo-Lun and my friends at Linworth who eagerly embraced and got behind my ideas for this book.

Finally, I would like to thank my family: my brother and his wife, Dr. & Mrs. Michael P. Nett for their photography contributions; my parents, Dr. & Mrs. Patrick A. Nett, for encouraging me to "get up and dance"; and my youngest brother, Joseph A. Nett, for providing me the inspiration to keep on writing, when I saw him working on his own writing. I would also like to thank my grandmother, Huguette A. Nett, for inspiring me to be a strong, resilient woman.

Internet-Based Student Research

Creating to Learn with a Step-by-Step Approach, Grades 5–12

Introduction

The Challenge: Using Technology to Help Your Students

- Has your school provided you with computer equipment and expected you to use it to the benefit of your students—without giving you any direction?

- Are you using computers in your classroom along with project-based learning, but still failing to get the results you want?

- Do you find yourself re-teaching material that students were supposed to learn while working on their computer projects?

Across the country, schools have been competing to get the latest and greatest technologies. They have put large amounts of money into technology budgets, investing in laptop programs and getting computers into each classroom. Building administrators have bragged to the community about all their new technology purchases and how the technology will get their students ready for the real world and motivate learning. Simply having these technologies available seemed to some administrators and community members a guarantee that the school would become a top school. They believed that simply getting the students laptops would help them get higher paying jobs and help them pass their AP exams. But the mere existence of these technologies does not guarantee that a "high tech" curriculum is any better than a "no tech" curriculum.

In August 2002 at the New York Talks Conference in Tarrytown, New York, the keynote speaker, Alan November, stated that the Benton Organization had completed an exhaustive study in which it found that $40 billion had been spent on technology—without any corresponding increase in student performance. Schools have bought hardware and software, spent money on wiring needs, and hired network administrators and IT professionals. They have hired technology directors to network computers, reformat hard drives, and operate Novell network systems. They started hiring instructional technology facilitators to "push in" to classrooms across multiple disciplines to help them infuse technology into their curriculums, but most of the time these personnel spend their time bombarded with hardware and software questions.

I have visited the most "technology advanced" schools in the country only to be disappointed. Some schools that bragged about their implementation of instructional technology had teachers using laptop or desktop computers with projectors and screens, showing students poorly-put-together presentations. Other schools were excited because their students all had remote controls that enabled them to answer quiz questions projected on a screen. Still other schools were excited because they had laptops for their students. Students could move around the room with their computers and create PowerPoint presentations that their instructional technology facilitator taught them to create: quickly locating Web pages, cutting and pasting information onto their slides, and animating their presentations.

None of these schools had developed a plan to infuse instructional technology into their curricula. They had not stopped to think how instructional technology could be used to help their students do better on their state and national exams. They didn't propose a plan to help teachers and instructional technology facilitators work together—to make the infusion of instructional technology into the curriculum meaningful for the students. I started to wonder…

What do we really want students to do with this new technology? How do we make sure students are using the technology to enhance their learning experience?

The power behind instructional technology is that it helps us discover and create things and then quickly share them with other people. Technology helps us build products like spreadsheets, publications, pictures, and movies. Technology helps us research information and share our own information. How can technology help us in the classroom? How can it help our students do better on their standardized tests? As teachers, we have core concepts that we need to cover with our students to prepare them for final exams and for state exams. How does instructional technology help us do that?

The essential question: *How is technology best utilized in good curriculum design?*

A Solution: The Creating to Learn Method

In search of an answer, I developed a methodology called the *Creating to Learn* method. The Creating to Learn method is an approach to learning that is grounded in discovery and active participation with any subject matter. It is successful because it encourages students to use their creative talents to forge a deeper understanding of a core concept. Students form an intimate experience with the subject matter, learning through active participation.

Creation is at the core of the Creating to Learn method—because creation is the cornerstone to more powerful and lasting learning.

Creating to Learn intertwines the creative process and the use of technology. Using this method, students create a finished product that provides evidence of their learning experience. We call this product a *knowledge entity* (see below). This deeper experience is what our students need to really understand their subject matter, to perform better on standardized tests, and to answer open-ended and critical-thinking questions about curriculum content.

What Is a Knowledge Entity?

A highly developed knowledge entity should have many aspects of activity and personal engagement. It shouldn't rest with any one aspect of learning like reading, writing, research, speaking or artwork; the most successful knowledge entities demonstrate a combination of many skills. While the actual knowledge entities are subject to the individuals' style, creativity, and sometimes even to their own interpretation, they must still represent learning within a finite curriculum.

Here are some examples of knowledge entities:

- **A professional newsletter.** Rather than more traditional letters to the editor or newspaper article assignments that have no design criteria, a more complete knowledge entity would be a "professional" newsletter. This forces the students to be writers, editors, graphic artists, design professionals, and perhaps even webmasters.

- **A motion picture project.** Rather than a skit to depict a historical event, a more sophisticated knowledge entity would be to film such a skit and then incorporate music, graphics, and images of original or historic artifacts. Using today's technology, students can easily edit and produce high-quality productions that will create invaluable experiences and learning journeys.

- **A study of exchange rates.** Rather than an isolated exercise of calculating a page of currency exchange rates while studying fractions in a math class, a more powerful knowledge entity would incorporate a complete study of exchange rates. Students could be assigned to look up the currency exchange rate between the Mexican peso and the U.S. dollar every day for a two-week period. Using a basic spreadsheet, students could record the daily exchange rates and calculate the price of goods in Mexico in terms of U.S. dollars, and chart the fluctuations on a line graph. This assignment allows more time to be spent critically analyzing the data and offers more visual tools to understand the dynamics of currency exchange.

Knowledge entities, such as those illustrated above, are the culmination of the successful implementation of the Creating to Learn method.

The Creating to Learn method

- employs instructional technology in a meaningful way, advancing creativity within the classroom;

- empowers students to take charge of their learning, wrapping every step of the process around curricular concepts;

- implements instructional technology in the curriculum, enabling students to create professional-quality knowledge entities demonstrative of their curricular insights and understandings;

- holds teachers accountable for understanding their curriculum matter;

- holds students accountable for taking an active role in their learning; and

- bridges the gap between using technology as a break from the curriculum and using it in support of the curriculum.

The CIDE Process

Concept

Concept: A basic idea that, when developed, guides you to a deeper understanding of the topic.

Design: Choosing appropriate media to represent ideas about the concept.

Investigation

Design

Investigation: Researching, organizing, and analyzing facts to better understand the concept.

Execution

Execution: Carrying out the planned design, to communicate ideas about the concept to others.

Keane, *Internet-Based Student Research: Creating to Learn with a Step-by-Step Approach* © 2005.

i-1 Introduction to the CIDE Process

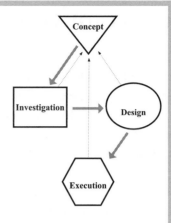

The Creating to Learn process will help you develop your research, organizational, visual, and technical skills, which in turn will help you not only with your projects, but also with all of your other studies.

The **CIDE** process breaks down projects into the following four phases:

Concept
Investigation
Design
Execution

You will notice that in the diagram the phases are connected to each other, with both solid and dotted lines. The thick solid-line arrows show you the order you should follow when putting together your project. (You always start with the Concept and then move to Investigation, Design, and finally Execution.) The thinner dotted-line arrows connect all the phases back to the Concept, reminding you that every step of the project is built around exploring that idea. As you work on your project, you must constantly remind yourself of the question you are answering.

Concept
This is the question that your teacher asked you to think about. Your project should answer this question. This is one of the most important parts of the CIDE process. It is the question you start with, and you keep revisiting that question throughout the CIDE process.

Investigation
This part of the process requires you to do research, to find out information that will help you answer the question your teacher and the library media specialist assigned. As you progress through your research, you should collect, classify, and sort your data using the tools provided to you with Microsoft Office. This can be a tricky part of the CIDE process. You must spend a lot of time on this phase to make sure you research your topic completely and correctly, and ensure that all of the information you are finding is accurate, by double-checking your sources. You should work closely with the library media specialist during this part of the project. He or she will be able to guide you and help you locate scholarly information.

Design
This part of the process asks you to plan how your project will be built, by creating a rough draft or scrap copy. You will decide what type of project to build and what design elements can be effective in various types of projects. You are creating a blueprint for your final project.

Execution
This last phase of the process is when you actually get to build your project. By following the blueprint you created in the Design phase, you express your answer to the teacher's question in a unique and creative way. The Execution phase is the creation phase: It is the realization of your own knowledge entity that answers the question posed in the Concept.

Using CIDE in Your Classroom

The Creating to Learn method guides us to deeper understanding of a subject by fostering personal experience. It has four essential phases that can be systematically applied in the classroom: Concept, Investigation, Design, and Execution (CIDE). The CIDE process leads us to explore a well-defined concept and build a personal lasting learning experience around that concept. It enhances the learning experience because understanding is developed through students' experiences; knowledge entities are indicative of students' insights, making learning "active, volitional," and "meaningful" (see p. 19).

A knowledge entity should encapsulate the whole creative process by demonstrating the personal learning journey encountered by the students as they explore the concept. Knowledge entities direct students on a learning journey that creates lasting experiences and durable memories. Learning is active, not passive.

Working through the Four Phases

1. Concept

> **Concept**
> A fundamental idea or premise that when cultivated guides the student to a deeper understanding of the subject matter.

As a systematic approach, the Creating to Learn method offers you a way to work through the process with your students, and the process always starts with a concept. The concept is critical for your students to understand. They will think about it, work with it, and mold it throughout the entire CIDE process, finally producing a creative expression of it. The students and the concept will go through a journey together in which the students create meaningful relationships that can be called upon at a later date and expanded upon throughout the rest of their lives.

Before Class: Choosing a Concept

As the educator, you extrapolate this core concept from the curriculum. To choose a concept, consider the following questions:

- What are the most pertinent points in your curriculum?
- What ideas or premises do you need your students to really understand?
- What concepts do your students need to think about, work with, and become intimate with?

Grant Wiggins and Jay McTighe in *Understanding by Design* (1998) identified "four criteria for determining when material is worthy not just of covering but of understanding. The material should be enduring, [be] at the heart of the discipline, need uncovering, and [be] potentially engaging" (p. 23).

> *A good* **Creating to Learn** *concept is*
> - essential to understanding the curriculum,
> - open-ended,
> - capable of growth, and
> - standards-based.

The First Day: Introducing the Concept

It is essential that you thoroughly describe the concept the students are exploring on the first day of the project:

1. Introduce the concept to the students. Write it on the board and discuss it. All the students should copy the concept into their learning journals and participate in the whole-class discussion.

2. The students should then independently create graphic organizers about the concept, including questions about the concept they want answered and any related ideas and interpretations. The students should keep these graphic organizers and their reflections with them throughout the project, for two purposes. First, they ensure that the students understand what you are asking of them. Second, they serve as a benchmark of the students' present understanding of the concept, which you can use to differentiate the lesson for the students throughout the remainder of the project.

3. Conclude the class with a reflection on the concept.

2. Investigation

> **Investigation**
> Exploring the concept through information collecting, classifying, sorting, abstracting, and analyzing.

During the Investigation phase, students should be doing the following:

*   Using the Internet to research the concept
*   Using textbooks and periodicals to research the concept
*   Talking to each other about the information they find online
*   Deciding if the information they've found is pertinent to the concept
*   Experimenting with simulations and collecting data about their findings
*   Preparing index cards and spreadsheets to collect their findings

As student become "infotectives," you may want to use this time to conference with them individually, to review their graphic organizers and their initial reflections on the concept.

Jamie McKenzie first used the term *infotective* in his book, *How Teachers Learn Technology Best*:

> Infotective is a term designed for education in an Age of Information. In the smokestack school, teachers imparted meaning for students to digest, memorize and regurgitate. In Information Age schools, students make the meaning. They puzzle their way through piles of fragments—sorting, sifting, weighing and arranging them until a picture emerges. These same skills produce high performance on the increasingly challenging state tests of reading comprehension and problem solving. As state standards require more and more inferential reasoning, state tests are asking students to "create answers" rather than "find answers." (1999, p. 41)

You can facilitate students' research by reviewing the Investigation section of this book. You may also want to guide your students through this phase with some pertinent questions, like these:

- Describe the concept you are exploring in your own words.
- Are there any other questions you have about your concept?
- What resources are available to help you with your research?
- How do you plan to organize your research?

This is a great time to collaborate with your library media specialists. Tell them about your project. Explain the concept to them and ask them what types of electronic databases and print sources the library might have available for you and your class to use.

3. Design

Design
Planning the form and scope of a knowledge entity.

Students must synthesize their investigation with their own unique talents and vision. They should re-read their investigations and use resources to plan their knowledge entities. The scope of the design, the blueprint for the knowledge entity, is indicative of the student's current understanding of the concept.

> Students must remember that research is meant to produce new ideas. This development of fresh answers may be the most difficult tasks of all. Smokestack schools often required little more than the collection and re-hashing of old ideas and discoveries. Student were rarely challenged to develop original insights. Now the research "game" has changed dramatically. Intrigued by an authentic question, students find themselves sorting and sifting through the data they have collected, arranging and rearranging the jigsaw pieces and fragments until some picture emerges. They are "on their own." No one shows them the picture on the puzzle box. (McKenzie, 1999, p. 52)

A design can be any of the items below, by themselves or in combination:
- An outline for a research paper
- A sketch of a publication, newsletter, or tri-fold brochure
- A storyboard for a movie
- A brainstorm list of pictures that are needed to create and share a moment in time

This design or blueprint provides an excellent opportunity for you to reflect with the students upon the scope of their investigations. Set up a checkpoint for your students. Require them to show you their blueprints, so you can make sure their designs are indicative of the concept. They should be prepared to answer questions about their designs and have a good understanding of the concept.

You may want to give the following questions to your students before their conferences, so they can prepare for their discussion with you. You may also want the students to reflect on these questions in their learning journals.

- Why did you decide to depict the concept as a publication, tri-fold, movie, etc.?
- What do you need to execute this design?
- Do you have a timetable to actualize each section of the design?
- Have you revisited the concept? Have you re-read the questions in your graphic organizer?
- How does your design reflect all the information you have obtained during the project?
- Has your understanding of the concept changed during your investigation? How is this reflected in your design?

4. Execution

> **Execution**
> Creating a reflection of the concept, investigation, and design in the form of a knowledge entity.

The knowledge entity should be the culmination of a learning journey, and it should demonstrate the personal experience unique to each student. The actualization of a final product to represent the student's experience with the concept is critical in ensuring the student has traveled the journey. Remember, each student learns and moves through the journey at a different pace.

Students in the Execution phase should be doing the following:

- Using their designs to actualize their knowledge entities
- Creating lists of things they need to actualize their designs (What hardware do we need? What software is best suited to make our knowledge entity?)
- Dividing the Execution phase into tasks, so each group member can take charge of a segment of the actualization of the product

You may want to provide students with a rubric like the one on the next page, so they can evaluate their own knowledge entities.

Rubric: The CIDE Process

The following rubric will be used to evaluate your final project, your knowledge entity.

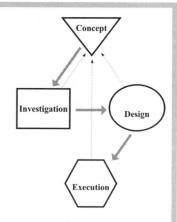

CIDE Rubric

Phase/Status	Not Yet	Okay	Excellent
Concept	The entity is not indicative of the concept.	The entity represents the concept, but it does not demonstrate that you came to a deeper understanding of the concept.	The entity is indicative of the concept and clearly demonstrates that you came to a deeper understanding of the concept.
Investigation	The knowledge entity does not demonstrate results from your investigation.	The knowledge entity demonstrates that you did minimal investigation.	The knowledge entity demonstrates that you did extensive investigation.
Design	The knowledge entity does not follow your design.	The knowledge entity reflects your original design.	The knowledge entity's execution caused your original design to change for the better. Your design was changed and now reflects the knowledge entity.
Execution	The knowledge entity shows no creativity and is not fully executed.	The knowledge entity is fully executed. It represents the concept, but lacks in true ingenuity.	The knowledge entity shows your unique talents and creativity: it could only have been created by you.

The Role of Instructional Technology

The successful integration of technology in the CIDE process requires students to demonstrate refined research, critical thinking, communication, and analytical skills. They will need to use these higher-order thinking skills to properly implement instructional technology while uncovering the concept.

Research skills and critical thinking skills go hand in hand when employing instructional technology in the Investigation phase. Students will need to analyze and extrapolate pertinent data related to their concept from the abundance of information available to them online and in print. The CIDE process requires that students learn fine-tuned research strategies so they can make better decisions (e.g., which search engines are most appropriate for their assignments). For a successful investigation, students must evaluate online information for authenticity. They need to dissect a Web page's URL address and explore the external hyperlinks attached to it to determine if the material is scholarly and reliable.

Communication skills are developed as students investigate their concept, not only working with classmates, but also e-mailing community members and experts in the field. You can help students develop their writing skills to help foster these authenticating relationships. Students will learn to clarify their thoughts in writing, to process their e-mail responses, and to build new knowledge from these communications. The students' communication skills are further developed when they begin to communicate their thoughts, feelings, arguments, and research with an assortment of visual and auditory expressions, including pictures, Web pages, movies, publications, diagrams, and concept maps. They learn good presentation skills, such as the effective use of visual teleprompts for their spoken word, the engagement of the audience with the topic, and a thorough understanding of the knowledge being shared.

Analytical skills are developed by using various tools, including spreadsheets like those created in Microsoft Excel. Spreadsheets can be used to perform complex mathematical operations and to store and manipulate data in various ways. The multifaceted manipulation of data augments the analytical process by helping students to view their information from different perspectives and extrapolate the information most pertinent to discovering the concept standards. For example, when students use Excel to store data, they can quickly change the data into charts or filter the data according to different parameters.

Instructional technology is the vehicle to move your students through the components of the CIDE process. But *you*, as the teacher, are the most important factor for the successful implementation of the CIDE process. You teach your students the higher-order thinking skills they need so they can use technology to discover the content standards.

Setting Up Your Classroom

There are many different forms of collaboration and cooperative learning that you can use. You are the best judge to determine what type of approach will work in your classroom. You need to develop a style that complements your teaching pedagogy and that suits your students' learning needs. Some classes might work well in groups of four while other classes might work best in partners and even still other classes might be better off working individually, collaborating only on their own time through e-mail. You need to decide what works best for you and your students.

Getting Started with Group Work

I have been most successful at building classrooms that enable students to work together and share their knowledge skills and build off of one another's strengths when I introduce group work slowly into the classroom setting. I usually like to do a lot a "teacher talk" in the beginning of the year, going over the rules and providing my students with an overview of the course. I feel it helps to set the academic tone for the rest of the year. I also find it extremely helpful to discuss with my students the most essential components of the curriculum at the beginning of the year, so they know where to focus their efforts.

Working as a Class

Then, I ease my students into a simple form of collaboration. We usually make something as a class. For example, each student might create one PowerPoint slide to be included in a class slide show. In this instance, the concept is introduced to the students on the first day of the project. Students are then provided some class time to investigate the concept after being introduced to some new search engines and learning how to authenticate Web pages. After completing their investigations, a mini-lesson is used to introduce the students to some of the key principles of design. Students first design their slides on paper. The following day is a quick tutorial on the key features of PowerPoint; students are given the remainder of the period to make their own slide. At the end of the unit, I use the class's presentation either as a review for the test or as a concluding lesson.

Working in Partners

I then introduce independent group work by having my students work in partners for a short amount of time. It might be only 30 seconds at first, to have them re-teach or review new material we just covered. This technique is helpful because it gets the students used to working together and sharing their understandings with one another. When working as a class and working in partners become second nature to the students, they can move on to a more complex level of collaboration: groups of four.

Working in Groups

Once you have the students working in groups of four, you can use those groups in two different capacities. Each group can work on a particular concept and create a knowledge entity together, or each group can be assigned different activities related to one project. For example, instead of you teaching the students the difference between a search engine, an online directory, and a metasearch engine and how to authenticate a Web site you might want to assign each of these tasks to a group. The first group studies search engines, while the second group works on online directories, the third group studies metasearch engines, and the fourth group learns how to authenticate and evaluate Web sites. All the groups use the information and handouts provided in this text to help guide their study. At the end of class, each group presents its findings to the rest of the class. In this case, your students have an opportunity to work in groups and teach each other, but they are still responsible for their own knowledge entity.

If cooperative learning and collaboration just don't work for you or your students, you can still use the Creating to Learn method. You can teach your students the difference between an online directory, search engine, and metasearch engine and how to validate a Web site. When I want to spearhead the lesson, I create a PowerPoint that hyperlinks to the different Web pages I want to show the students. I connect my laptop to a projector and show the students how to do a thorough Web investigation. This book is filled with handouts that students can complete after you have finished the lesson.

This book draws on the different talents of students and is made to work with many different types of teachers. Teachers teach best not when they employ a certain teaching style or methodology, but when they use the style that works best for them. Therefore, you should continue using whatever teaching style you have already been successful with in the classroom, but try updating that style with a few new ideas and lessons from this guide.

A Better Classroom Experience

Students using the creative (CIDE) process have the opportunity to develop, grow, and invent new ideas throughout their schooling. This learning model will also serve them in problem-solving and creative-thinking situations outside the classroom environment. It teaches students to take concepts rooted in their traditional standardized curriculum and cultivate them into personal knowledge entities that represent learning experiences in which they clarify, research, and creatively demonstrate their growth and learning with the assistance of cutting-edge technology. Students are trained to complement their creative thinking with keenly polished presentation and communication skills that add quality and richness to their work.

The Creating to Learn method produces

- enthusiastic and accomplished students,

- teachers who have more latitude in their assignments,

- administrators who can be proud of the use of their cutting-edge technology, and

- communities that enjoy rewarding and symbiotic relationships with their schools.

Planning Your Project

On the opposite page is a table with a suggested time line for the completion of a knowledge entity. But for each teacher, teaching style, and learning style, the project will unfold uniquely. Don't worry if you can't follow the time allotted in the table. You should probably develop your own timetable for your project, depending on the complexity of your concept and topic. The table is here as a guide only.

For instance, if the concept is the cornerstone of your curriculum and is essential to understanding the rest of the curriculum, you may want to spend some substantial time developing your knowledge entities. You need to ask yourself before beginning the project, "How important is this concept to the heart of the subject matter?" If the concept is truly the cornerstone in the curriculum, you may want to dedicate the entire year to exploring it. That doesn't mean that you work on it every day, but that it would be an ongoing project.

You might want to review this timetable with your library media specialists as well. Invite the library media specialists into your classroom to help you with the Investigation phase. Ask them how many days they would need to work with you and your students.

This table outlines the stages that you go through with your students when creating a knowledge entity and also estimates the amount of time that could be spent at each stage. Again, the table is a guide and may change according to your teaching style and your students' learning needs.

Time-Saving Tips

1. **Use software your students already know.** If your students are used to using Inspiration® instead of CmapTools™, use Inspiration. They are both great mind-mapping tools.

2. **Use outside class time.** Older students can complete a lot of their research at home after learning a few key tips about searching the Internet.

3. **Create deadlines and milestones**. I can't stress how important it is to spot-check your students' progress throughout the project. You also may want to give your students separate deadlines to complete the Investigation and Design phases. This will save you time in the end.

4. **Make sure your students know how to save their work correctly!** Many students don't have any practice in file management. They need to create a folder for the knowledge entity on their computer and save all their work for the project there. You don't want students saving their work all over the school's network; they may never be able to locate it again.

Suggested Time Line for Completing a Knowledge Entity

Stage	Est. Time	Recommended Handouts
Before the project starts: • Introduction to the unit and to the personal journal • Introduction to the CIDE process and the concept	2–3 days	i-1 Introduction to the CIDE Process
Prewriting, brainstorming, and concept mapping	2 days (1 to learn the software and 1 to prewrite)	Handouts on CmapTools™ software. I-1 Your Research Process Diagram
Investigation • Introduction to library media specialist • Explanation of online databases and print resources • Introduction to online databases • Explanation of targeted searching • Introduction to the visible and invisible Web • Authentication • Organization	6–7 days	Popular Online Directories Table I-2 Online Directories I-3 Reflect on Online Browsing I-4 Boolean Operators I-5 Reflect on Search Engines I-6 Reflect on Metasearch Engines I-7 Reflect on the Invisible Web I-8 The Top 10 Online Searching Strategies I-9 Reflect on the Investigation Section Research Checklist Savvy Investigation Checklist
Design: Explanation of project choices	1 day	Project Choices Checklist
Global design principles	3–4 days	D-1 Choosing the Right Medium D-2 Introduction to Design D-3 Location, Location, Location! D-4 Redirecting a Reader's Attention D-5 Types of Visual Expression D-6 Choosing Font Types and Attributes Global Design Principles Checklist
Blueprints: Creating thumbnail sketches, storyboards, and albums	3–5 days	D-7 Outlines: Organizing Your Presentation D-8 Dissecting a Newsletter D-9 Creating a Magazine Cover Page D-10 Learning to Become a Photographer D-11 A Photographer's Journal Sample storyboards
Spot-checks of outlines, sketches, and storyboards/albums	1 day	Project Blueprint Checklist
Execution: Putting together the final project, assessment and testing	5 days	E-1 Delivering Your Presentation E-2 Tips for Better Digital Photography Any other instructions to help your students complete their knowledge entities.
Concluding activities	1–3 days	
Total class time	**24–31 days**	

The Theoretical Basis for CIDE

Using the Scientific Method to Meet Educational Standards

The basis of the CIDE process is really nothing new or profound—in fact, it has been largely accepted and used as standard scientific practice since the early 1600s. Back then, it was a radical approach to science. Earlier approaches had relied on the Bible for truths, while this new approach was based in observation and experimentation: It tested ideas before converting them into scientific truths and laws. Eventually this new approach was refined into seven steps and became known as the *scientific method*:

1. State the problem.
2. Gather information on the problem.
3. Form a hypothesis (or educated guess).
4. Experiment to test the hypothesis.
5. Record and analyze data.
6. State a conclusion.
7. Repeat the steps.

The CIDE process follows the same line of reasoning. Students are challenged with a concept, and they investigate the challenge, problem, or essential question. As their investigations progress, they challenge their hypothesis, their original beliefs, and even their own intuitions. Then the students reflect on their investigations, analyze their discoveries, and design knowledge entities that represent their new findings and own unique understandings.

Testing CIDE in the Field

Following in the footsteps of our Renaissance forefathers, I experimented with the CIDE process with students, other teachers, and administrators. The process was field-tested at Suffern High School, New York, and at Wareham Middle School, Massachusetts.

At Suffern High School, the CIDE process was used across the curriculum: in health, social studies, language arts, and science classrooms. Teachers and students (grades 9–12) used the model to help them successfully implement a student-centered learning environment that focused on state standards and mandates. The model innately prepared students for their New York State Regents exams by connecting the concept of each knowledge entity to the New York State standards and the major curricular subjects.

At Wareham Middle School, the model was field-tested in a full-inclusion language arts/social studies classroom. The CIDE process intrinsically differentiated instructions for the different learners in the classroom, while developing their critical-thinking skills and preparing them for the Massachusetts Comprehensive Assessment System (MCAS) exam.

Meeting State and Federal Regulations

The CIDE process is a perfect fit for high-stake classrooms that are focused on state and federal regulations and are subject to state and federal testing requirements, especially since the No Child Left Behind (NCLB) federal legislation. Schools are now expected to demonstrate continuous and substantial academic improvement for all students. States are required to have a time line with a starting point, intermediate goals, annual measurable objectives, and academic indicators. (34 CFR § 200.5)

The CIDE process helps students develop higher-order thinking skills and deeper understandings based on mandated state curriculum concepts. It intertwines active learning with state expectations, thereby creating an environment in which all students learn and are engaged in the subject matter. This intimate relationship between the CIDE process and state standards enables high student performance on state exams and ensures that schools meet and exceed state indicators on their NCLB time lines.

Not only does the CIDE process help the classroom teacher and the library media specialist surpass national and state learning standards by focusing students' course of study on the most essential points of the curriculum, but it also helps this resource team meet and exceed the National Educational Technology Standards (NETS) for students. These are standards based on the International Standard in Technology Education (ISTE) for teachers and library media specialists, describing what students should know and be able to do with technology.

The NETS have six basic strands of beliefs regarding how students should be using instructional technology. They include the following ideas: students using technology proficiently; students using technology to enhance learning and promote creativity; and students using technology to locate, evaluate, and collect information from different sources.

The CIDE process supports and enhances these standards by promoting information literacy skills such as accessing information efficiently and evaluating information in the Investigation phase. It further supports these national standards by requiring students to use technology creatively in the Design phase and by teaching students to use technology proficiently, in the Execution phase.

The Learning Process

A vast quantity of research and many educational philosophers and teachers support the need to have a systematic visual learning model that promotes students' active participation in their learning environment. For example, the American Psychological Association's Presidential Task Force on Psychology in Education circulated the fourth draft of its *Learner-Centered Psychological Principles: Guidelines for School Redesign and Reform* in January 1993. Principle 1 in the task force's study defines "the nature of the learning process":

> Learning is a natural process of pursuing personally meaningful goals. It is active, volitional, and internally motivated; it is a process of discovering and constructing meaning from information and experience, filtered through the learners' unique perceptions, thoughts, and feelings. Students are capable of assuming personal responsibility for their own learning if the educational situation takes into account their past learning, ties the new learning to personal goals, and actively involves the students in the learning process. (Woolfolk, 1995, p. 479)

The CIDE process is the manifestation of the idea expressed in the first principle of the APA's study. It takes this principle and forms a visual systematic model providing a structure in which each student actively participates, thinks through problems to investigate and solve them, and finally produces a knowledge entity out of their own "volition."

Good Instructional Design

The APA's study is further supported by the findings in Jane Lynch's article "Constructivism and Distance Learning." In this article, Lynch articulates the constructivist theorists' definition of "good instructional design." According to a constructivist, good instructional design creates an environment that promotes students' connections of old information to new information through interaction with others. It allows them time to actually construct the new knowledge in their brains (Lynch, 1997).

Furthermore, constructivist theorists define the successful classroom setting as a learning experience where the teacher facilitates student-led investigations, projects, and conversations, providing students the opportunity to build from one another's ideas, constructing new kernels of knowledge. The CIDE process depends on the teacher's ability to uncover curricular concepts, facilitate student-led investigations, and work with students using technology to produce creations expressive of their understanding.

Having a systematic model to follow helps teachers ensure that their students are constructing new knowledge around the fundamental concepts in their curriculum. The CIDE process provides a map for teachers to design their lessons and projects. It is a visual model of "good instructional design" providing a road map for teachers.

Advanced Thinking Required

The CIDE process breaks learning into four distinct phases. These phases ensure that students interact with others during the Investigation phase while they hunt and gather new ideas about old information. The new ideas are connected to old information during the Design phase, as students think critically about the information and synthesize ideas. New ideas are brought to fruition during the Execution phase. In a constructivist classroom setting, good instructional design such as the CIDE process facilitates student-led investigations, project-based learning, and student interaction. This kind of classroom environment promotes original thinking and offers new opportunities to experience learning.

Students learn not only by being active in their learning but also by using advanced thinking skills. As described by Benjamin Bloom in his taxonomy of the cognitive domain, thinking skills can be classified at six different levels: knowledge, comprehension, application, analysis, synthesis, and evaluation. Many teachers use these levels of their students' understanding to design their lesson plans, units, and assessments. The better students understand an idea, the higher-order critical thinking skills they can apply to it. The CIDE process works within the highest range of skills, requiring students to apply, analyze, synthesize, and evaluate material, thus gaining a deeper understanding of the subject matter:

- **Application** – Students call on previous knowledge and skills to develop, design, and create knowledge entities.
- **Analysis** – Students investigate and validate material they've gathered during the Investigation phase. They need to analyze and abstract pertinent data from frivolous information; they also need to evaluate the data in relationship to their concepts and synthesize the data.
- **Synthesis** – In the Design phase, students foster synthesis skills while creating blueprints that combine their learning with personal experiences, demonstrating deeper, new understandings.
- **Evaluation** – Students must constantly evaluate their projects to ensure that all the phases are directed toward the initial concept.

Intelligence and Creativity

J.P. Guilford's work in multiple intelligences suggests there are three basic categories, or faces, of intellect: "mental operations" (the process of thinking), "contents" (what we think about), and "products" (the end result of our thinking). According to Guilford, carrying out a cognitive task is essentially performing a mental operation on some specific content to achieve a product (Woolfolk, 1995, p. 110). The CIDE process helps students do just that. It gives them a road map that will take them from a visual or mental operation to an entity demonstrative of their unique understandings. Students have the latitude to use their own unique or multiple intelligences to bring their ideas to actualization.

Another theorist in the area of multiple intelligences is Howard Gardner. Gardner theorizes that there are eight multiple intelligences in which individuals can be gifted; therefore, students learn and process information in multiple ways, depending on their areas of intelligence (Woolfolk, 1995, p. 111). Many students are naturally inclined to use the stronger aspects of their intelligence to accomplish tasks, but they need a fuller understanding of the direction their talents should be driven. It is our job as educators to help students identify, define, and develop their own uniqueness in a positive and productive manner. The CIDE process offers students a method for developing their own special creative niche, with its systematic approach to creative thinking.

Creativity is one of the cornerstones to developing our students' academic talents. Robert Sternberg bases his Triarchic Theory of Intelligence on students' ability to be flexible, invent, and make new products. "Sternberg's triarchic theory suggests that intelligent behavior is the product of applying thinking strategies, handling new problems creatively and quickly, and adapting to contexts by selecting and reshaping our environment" (Woolfolk, 1995, p. 114). The CIDE process works well by these parameters of intelligence because it provides a structure to think through problems, investigate, and problem solve. It goes even further when students demonstrate their intelligence by creating a well-conceived knowledge entity.

In helping students create a knowledge entity, *Internet-Based Student Research: Creating to Learn with a Step-by-Step Approach* also supports the *Understanding By Design* philosophy (Wiggins and McTighe, 1998). It provides students a systematic process to follow, guiding them through each step with a specific end in mind. Students are charged with essential questions to explore, uncovering the "big ideas" embedded in the curriculum. This active learning/creating gives students an experience in which to base their investigations and develop their concepts.

New Skills

Like Sternberg, David Thornburg heavily emphasizes adaptability. In Thornburg's *The New Basics: Education and the Future of Work in the Telematic Age* (2002), he identifies and outlines the skills that students need to work on in the 21st century. He states that students will be required to adapt to their surroundings and be resourceful and creative just to keep pace with the new technological advances. The CIDE process offers a systematic process that leads students from concept to product. Once students learn the CIDE process, they will have a systematic road map to follow whenever adapting to new surroundings.

Thornburg says that students need to be equipped with four basic skills upon entering the workforce: technical literacy, invention, effective communication, and production. The Creating to Learn approach helps students use technology to invent and create products more efficiently and with professional quality. They learn the technical "how to" of commonly used educational software, along with the reasoning why technology should be employed to improve productivity. They use technology to journal new conceptions; to accelerate, broaden, and validate investigative sources; to improve their designs; and to execute professional-quality products.

Similar to David Thornburg, Ted McCain and Ian Jukes address the skill sets that students will need to succeed in the 21st century. In their book *Windows on the Future: Education in the Age of Technology* (2002), Jukes and McCain describe how the evolving nature of technology and the versatility and flexibility expected of employees demand new skill sets. They believe that students need to be equipped with a systematic creative process for problem solving and critical thinking; they also need to be flexible, to be able to continually adapt as their surroundings change. Jukes states that the workplace requires employees who are information-literate, who are effective communicators, and who maintain their technical reading and writing skills. *Internet-Based Student Research: Creating to Learn with a Step-by-Step Approach* integrates these new skill sets, focusing on technical reading, research skills, and data organization. Equipped with these skills, students will eagerly tackle new technologies and enthusiastically welcome change as a starting point for new concepts in the CIDE process.

Internet-Based Student Research: Creating to Learn with a Step-by-Step Approach helps teachers help their students become information-literate. It also provides teachers an easy way to incorporate technical expertise in their classroom and to provide their students with experience in reading and following technical manuals. *Internet-Based Student Research: Creating to Learn with a Step-by-Step Approach*, with its many pages that can be copied as student handouts, is an ideal manual for teachers of the new millennium.

Works Cited

Lynch, E. (1997). Constructivism and distance education. Retrieved February 5, 2005, from http://seamonkey.ed.asu.edu/~mcisaac/emc703old97/spring97/7/lynch7.htm.

McCain, T., & Jukes, I. (2002). *Windows on the future: Education in the age of technology*. Thousand Oaks, CA: Corwin Press.

McKenzie, J. (1999). *How teachers learn technology best*. Bellingham, WA: FNO Press.

Thornburg, D. (2002). *The new basics: Education and the future of work in the telematic age*. Alexandria, VA: Association for Supervision and Curriculum Development.

Wiggins, G., & McTighe, J. (1998). *Understanding by design*. Alexandria, VA: Association for Supervision and Curriculum Development.

Woolfolk, A. E. (1995). *Educational psychology*. 6th ed. Boston: Simon & Schuster.

Investigation

The Information Constructivist

So what is an *information constructivist*? Let's break it down.

> *Information* means one of two things:
> 1. Something told — news
> 2. Facts learned — knowledge

> A *constructivist* is someone who works with others to build things.

The *information constructivist* then is a person who finds information gathered by others—in books, in periodicals, and online—then sorts, analyzes, and evaluates that information to create new ideas and obtain new knowledge.

A tech-savvy information constructivist can quickly obtain information from the Internet and then use computer software to help store, sort, and analyze that information.

Why is it important that your students become tech-savvy information constructivists?

Consider this from Alan November's powerful 1998 article, "Teaching Zack to Think":

> A 14-year-old Zack was writing a history paper about the Holocaust—specifically, about how it never actually happened. When asked about his topic, Zack said he read that the Holocaust never happened, on a Web page at Northwestern University.

> November explains that students are being taught to access the Internet to do research, but they are not being taught how to validate the information they find. "The Internet is a place where you can find 'proof' of essentially any belief system that you can imagine. And, for too many students, 'If it is on the Internet, it is true.'" (¶1)

Students need instruction in not only how to research topics on the Internet, but also how to analyze and evaluate the information they find.

With this section of *Internet-Based Student Research: Creating to Learn with a Step-by-Step Approach*, you can help your students focus on analyzing their topics and then researching them effectively online and evaluating the sources where they obtain their information.

Coming Up Next:
- The Information Challenge
- Research on the Internet
- Organization

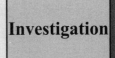

Investigation

1. The Information Challenge

Assigning students a research paper in the electronic age can be overwhelming with all the new online resources available. The key is to break down the research paper for your students, one step at a time.

The first step to helping your students successfully meet the information challenge posed to them is not writing, but rather *prewriting*.

The first step in the writing process: *Prewriting*

- Selecting and developing your subject
- Thinking, brainstorming, talking, and information collecting—before you start writing

From *Write Source 2000: A Guide to Writing, Thinking, and Learning* by P. Sebranek, D. Kemper, and V. Meyer, 1999, p. 46.

Use prewriting exercises when you introduce the concept to your students in a whole-class discussion, as described in the Introduction. Spend 10 to 15 minutes discussing the concept. Then devote the remainder of the class period to prewriting exercises and encourage the students to talk about the concept among themselves.

A number of prewriting activities are available to you. You can choose one of the whole-class prewriting activities suggested below or you can list the prewriting activities on the board and have students choose which work best for them. Dr. Alvin Baron, in *Bud's Easy Research Paper Computer Manual* (2002), suggests the following prewriting activities:

- Writing a personal journal
- Free writing
- Brainstorming keywords
- Clustering or mapping

Dr. Baron defines a *personal journal* as an opportunity for your students to begin listing ideas, questions, issues, quotations, summaries of newspaper articles, and notes about television programs. The journal helps students track their ideas freely, without worrying about their punctuation and grammar. Students start the journal in class and then continue at home; they should have a week or so to work on the journals at home before the project begins. Encourage your students to keep their journals throughout the entire project—adding ideas, sketches, notes, Web pages, and other new items that pertain to their concepts and, in the larger context, to their entire projects.

Free writing is an opportunity to write quickly about a topic without trying to zero in on a specific approach. It is an opportunity for students to free associate and let their ideas flow without stopping.

Coming Up Next:
- Diagram the Research Topic
- Tracking Ideas Visually

Investigation

This is a good time to invite the library media specialist into your classroom. Do the prewriting activity with the library media specialist in the room with you, so the students will see you working together from the beginning of the project, as a resource team. You might also invite the library media specialist to do a separate mini-lesson about identifying helpful keywords when searching for a topic online. After the mini-lesson, the two of you can circulate the room and help the students with their prewriting.

As the topic becomes more familiar to your students, they should be able to *brainstorm* to develop a list of keywords.

You may want to do this as a whole-class discussion. Have students review their personal journals and their free writing activities before asking for volunteers to write keywords on the board.

Main Keywords
The Renaissance and Reformation

Additional Brainstormed Words
Protestant Reformation
The Scientific Revolution
Art and Literature
Humanism

Brainstorming keywords

Diagram the Research Topic

So you and your class have decided to embark on a project-based research assignment, but you still don't know how to get your students started? There are so many choices, so many possible paths to take. With all these ideas and questions floating around, it is sometimes easier to use a visual aid.

A simple diagram called a *graphic organizer* can help your students organize their ideas and any questions they may have about their concept. It can help you and your classes break down the research assignment into smaller, more manageable pieces.

Dr. Baron uses graphic organizers in *clustering and mapping*, to find major topics and subtopics. Jamie McKenzie also believes in the potential of graphical organizers:

> As powerful electronic networks provide students with access to mountains of information, graphical organizers convert complex and messy information collections into meaningful displays. Graphical organizers have become an essential weapon in the struggle against info-glut and info-garbage. They compress. They focus. They make interpretation, understanding, and insight much easier. Graphical organizers help students plan their research forays. They guide the gathering. They focus purpose. They show what is gained. They show what is still missing. Graphical organizers sometimes serve as mind maps. They point to the destination. They identify related sites and sights. They help students to stay on track.

> The new information landscape is laced with potential for frustration and disappointment as well as opportunities, as the new abundance is often offset by disorganization. Equipped with the right tools and skills, fortunately, students can find meaning and develop insight despite the disorder. (1997)

In *Internet-Based Student Research: Creating to Learn with a Step-by-Step Approach*, the graphic organizer is used as a primary tool that students use to track their ideas and their questions about a concept. The organizer also helps students categorize these ideas and questions into major topics and subtopics. As students progress in the Investigation phase, they will add new ideas and information to their graphic organizers.

Review the sample diagram below. You may want to share this sample with your class, either on the board or as a handout. Using this as an example, have the students start working on their own research process diagrams: Handout I-1.

Here's how it works:

1. Students write their topic, idea, concept statement in the center bubble of the visual diagram.

2. Students write any related details or questions they have about the topic in the bubbles branching off of the center bubble.

Sample Research Process Diagram

Main Topic

Civilizations experience times of wealth, intellectual growth, and discovery; they also experience times of great despair.

Related Subtopics and Questions

- What causes a society to experience a period of wealth, intellectual growth, and discovery?
- Why do some societies enjoy multiple growth periods while others remain in despair?
- What causes a society to fall after a period of rapid growth?

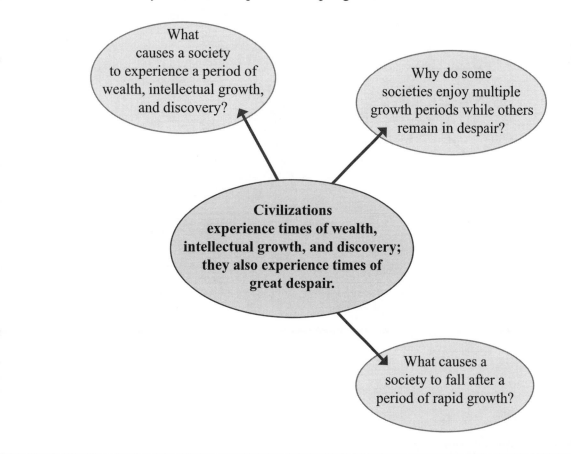

I-1 Your Research Process Diagram

Directions: Use the diagram below to begin prewriting.

Write your research topic in the center bubble. Then fill in each connected bubble with a related subtopic, question, or phrase. (It's okay if you have more than four subtopics. Just draw more bubbles.)

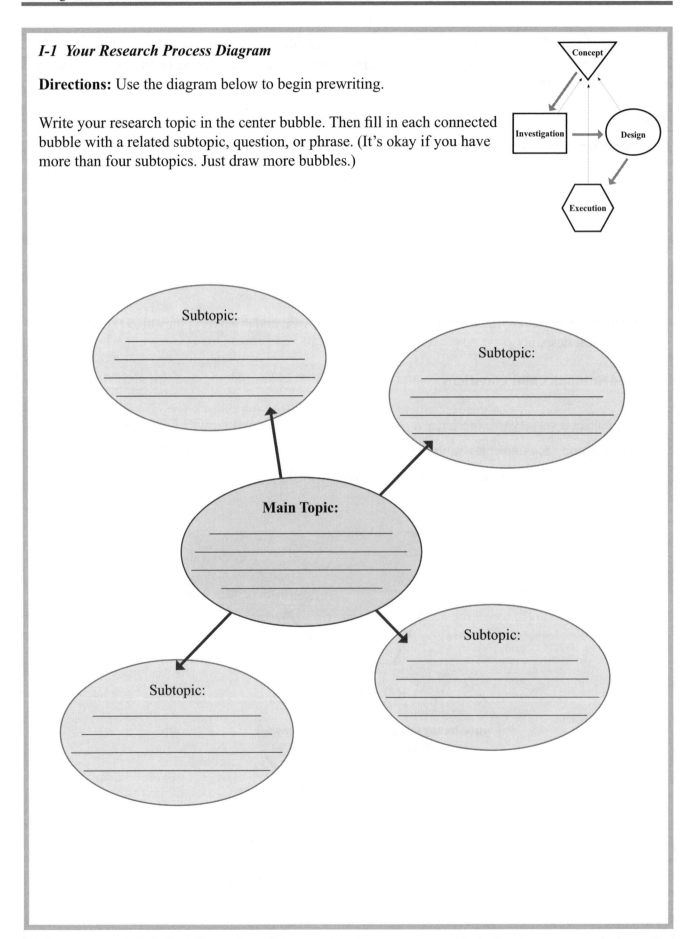

Keane, *Internet-Based Student Research: Creating to Learn with a Step-by-Step Approach* © 2005.

Tracking Ideas Visually

Help from CmapTools™

CmapTools™ is a great tool to introduce to your students. With this freeware, they can construct graphic organizers on their personal computers. According to its Web site (http://cmap.ihmc.us), the CmapTools program "empowers users to construct, navigate, share, and criticize knowledge models represented as Concept Maps." As students become more proficient in its use, they can share their graphic organizers on the CmapTools servers, link their maps to other Cmaps on the servers, automatically create Web pages of their concept maps, and even edit their maps at the same time with other users on the Internet! It is a cool tool that will help your students create and share their own graphic organizers, as well as view other graphic organizers that have been created about their topics.

Play around with the program to familiarize yourself with its features and capabilities. Here are some basic instructions to get you and your students started:

1. Type "http://cmap.ihmc.us" in the Internet Explorer address bar to access the CmapTools Web site.

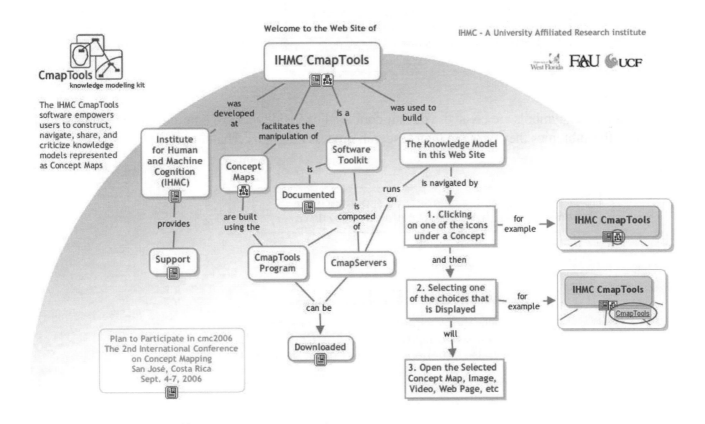

2. Double-click the "Downloaded" circle in the bottom center of the home page.

 This icon will bring you to an adjoining Web page where you can read more about CmapTools and download the appropriate version to your computer. For example, if you are using Windows XP, you should select the Windows version; if you are using a Macintosh operating system, you should select the Mac version.

3. After the software has been downloaded to your computer's desktop, you can start the installation process by double-clicking on the icon. You then follow the prompts for installing the software.

4. Once the program is installed, you can open CmapTools and start a new Cmap file.

5. Double-click in the center of the page where it says "double-click to create a concept." That's where you and your students should type the information challenge.

6. Then click and drag the arrow on top of the main topic symbol to make links for subtopics.

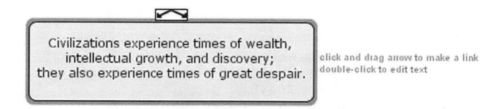

7. Once the other symbols are created, you can double-click inside them to edit the text. Students should type in the subtopics they wrote in their research process diagrams (Handout I-1).

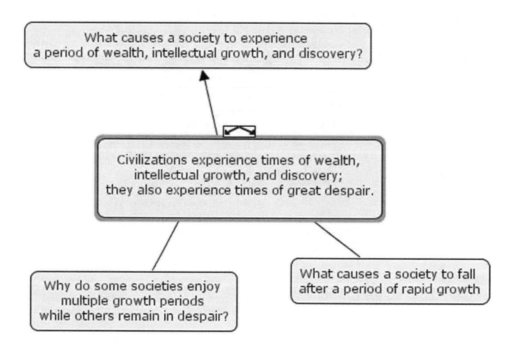

2. Research on the Internet

The Internet is a great source of information for both you and your students. It is loaded with Web pages, online directories, scholarly material, electronic journals, newsletters, electronic texts, online discussion forums, graphics, sounds, software, and even an invisible Web. But where in the world do you start? And how do you teach your students where to start?

This chapter explains Internet search tools and provides hints to help you and your students find online information related to any topic.

Research on the Internet is divided into two different categories: *browsing* and *searching*.

Remember: **Browsing is different than searching.**

To browse is to examine in a casual way.
vs.
To search is to examine thoroughly
by piercing and penetrating.

*(See the next page for more detailed information,
so you clearly explain it to your students.)*

Your students' first step to online research should always be browsing through an online directory such as Yahoo! or the Google Directory™.

What Is an Online Directory?

Online directories are a good way for students to begin learning more about their concept or topic. These directories are created by subject matter experts that categorize Web pages by their topics.

Online directories are organized in a hierarchy, from general to more specific topics, so they make finding information easy. Dr. Baron describes them like the branches of a tree. "Users can search from general to increasingly more specific topics" (2002, p. 1-42).

Browsing these online directories first can help your students identify the best keywords to use in their targeted searches and thereby be more efficient in their research.

Coming Up Next:
- Browsing Online Directories
- Targeted Searches
- The Visible and Invisible Web
- Authentication

Investigation

Browsing vs. Searching

So what's the difference?

You may want to take a few minutes of class time to explain to your students the difference between browsing for information online and searching for it.

> **Browse:**
> To examine in a casual way

Chris Sherman and Gary Price, in their book *The Invisible Web: Uncovering Information Sources Search Engines Can't See*, define *browsing* as "the process of following a hypertext trail of links created by other Web users. A hypertext link is a pointer to another document, image, or other object on the Web. The words making up the link are the title or description of the document that you will retrieve by clicking on the link. By its very nature, browsing the Web is both easy and intuitive" (2001, p. 19).

Online directories allow you and your students to casually look for information about their topics. *Browsing* directories can help your students identify the best keywords to use when they start *searching* for information about their topics.

> **Search:**
> To examine thoroughly
> by piercing and penetrating

Searching relies on powerful software that seeks to match the keywords you specify with the most relevant documents on the Web.

"Effective searching, unlike browsing, requires learning how to use the search software—as well as lots of practice—to develop skills to achieve satisfactory results" (Sherman & Price, 2001, p. 19).

Browsing Online Directories

Although each online directory will look a little different, in general, you will see a list of major topics on its home page. For example, the Google Directory™ begins with general topics, such as Arts, Business, and Computers, with subtopics under each of the general topics.

In order to access the Google Directory™ Web directory, type "www.google.com" in the Internet Explorer address bar and then select "more" on top of Google's search box. You will see a list of the Google Directory™ Web directory services. Click on "Directory."

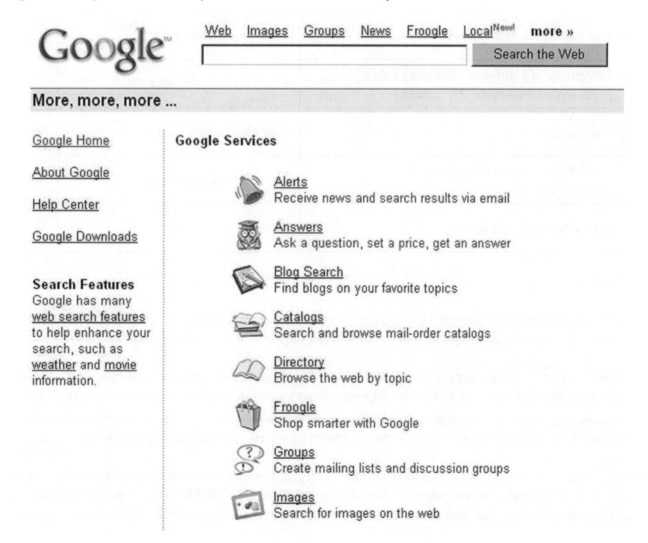

Popular Online Directories

After introducing your students to directories spend the next 20 minutes or so introducing other popular online directories. Have your students browse each of the directories identified by Dr. Baron in the table below. As they are browsing these online directories students should complete Handout I-2 to track the information they are gathering while browsing for their topics using some of these online directories.

Popular Online Directories

Online Directory Name	URL Address
Yahoo!	http://www.yahoo.com
Excite	http://excite.com
Google	http://directory.google.com
The Argus Clearinghouse	http://www.clearinghouse.net
The WWW Virtual Library	http://www.vlib.org
University of California, Berkeley Library (with Internet resources by subject)	http://lib.berkeley.edu
LookSmart	http://looksmart.com
INFOMINE: Scholarly Internet Resource Collections	http://infomine.ucr.edu
Librarians' Internet Index	http://www.lii.org

Note: In most directories you can also conduct directory searches to quickly locate information about your topic that is already categorized in the pre-linked online topics created by experts and volunteers.

Students' objective at this stage is to develop a list of keywords about their topic. If they find a great article, they should bookmark it, but should remember to focus on browsing through the hyperlinks.

Distribute Handout I-2 to your students. Provide them about 10 minutes to complete the handout.

Once you and your students learn how to conduct a targeted search, you should develop search strategies that help you penetrate the overwhelming amount of information available to them on the Internet. This will help your students find significant information related to their topics and be more efficient about it.

I-2 Online Directories

Directions: When you are first browsing for your research topic using an online directory, use this template to help track how experts on the Web categorize your subject.

1. Re-read your prewriting diagram and write your information challenge here—in your own words:

   _____

   _____

   _____

2. Write the names and URL addresses of two online directories that you plan to use to browse for your subject:

Online Directory Name	URL Address
1.	
2.	

3. Write the major categories and subcategories where you find your subject:

Online Directory	Major Category	Subtopics
1.		
2.		

Defining Your Keywords

As students browse through the directories, they should keep a running list of the categories they clicked through to find information on their topics. They may want to record these terms for future searches by adding notes to their Cmap symbols.

1. Select the symbol to which you want to add notes. You know the symbol is selected when you see a light blue outline.

2. Click on the symbol and hold down the Ctrl key. A pop-up menu will appear. Select "Add Notes."

3. Add the searchable terms identified while browsing in the "Mouse Over Info" or "Hidden Info" notes section. Mouse-over information displays the information when you hover your mouse over the symbol; hidden information can be searched when a search is conducted on key phrases or terms.

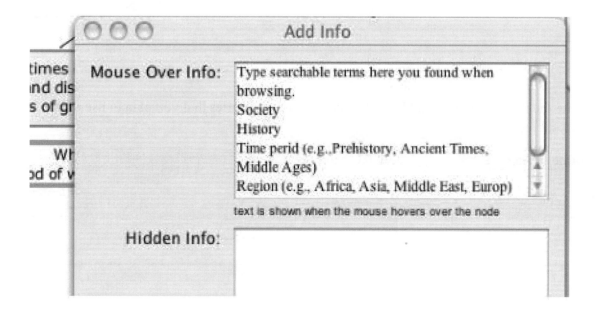

Continue to have your students browse through the online directories, identifying key terms that are related to their topics and the concept. Students should toggle between the online directory Web page and their Cmap organizer to record the key terms as they find them.

As students begin to learn more about their topics, they may feel it is necessary to add more subtopics to their main ideas. This is a normal part of the research process. They should add these subtopics to their Cmap organizer with the new symbol icon.

Create new symbol icon

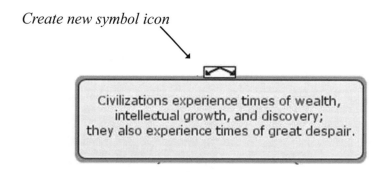

Color-Coordinate to Help Organize Your Ideas

Students may want to examine and indicate relationships between their questions and subtopics and the information problem by color-coordinating them with the CmapTools software.

To mark symbols of the same category the same color:

1. Right-click on the symbol.

2. Select "Format Style" from the pop-up menu.

3. Use the Color palette from the Styles pop-up menu to choose a color.

Students could use different colors to identify the different parts of their research paper. For example, they may want to use purple on all the symbols that are questions. They may want to color all the subtopics about one major issue in red.

Color bar

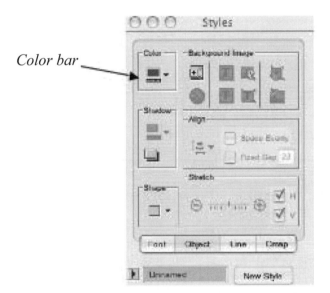

Distribute the Reflect on Online Browsing handout (Handout I-3) to your students. Have them complete it when they have finished browsing for information on their topic.

I-3 Reflect on Online Browsing

Directions: Think about the following questions when you write your reflections about this process below:

- *After you browsed online for your subject, did you learn anything unexpected?*

- *Is your subject still a good subject for your paper?*

- *What additional questions came to your mind as you started finding hyperlinks related to your subject?*

- *Has the main objective in your subject changed as a result of your online browsing?*

Reflections:

_____

_____

_____

_____

_____

_____

_____

_____

_____

_____

_____

_____

_____

_____

Targeted Searches

Searching the Web Efficiently

Both you and your students are probably already familiar with the Search boxes on the Internet. You type in whatever topic you're looking for, and Presto! A list of Web pages about that topic pops up on your computer screen.

But there's a problem. As you have probably already experienced, a simple one-word query can produce thousands of sites! There is no way you or your students could read all the Web pages and their hyperlinks. And the number of sites on the Internet is growing each day. How do you find what you're looking for? And how do your students find what they are looking for?

For example, if you and your students were studying China's two golden ages, you might conduct a search on "China's two golden ages." You would get many results that talked about the two golden ages of China, but you would also get a lot of results that referred to just China or golden, and every description imaginable of China, golden, ages, and two.

You and your students need to be able to quickly locate Web pages with relevant information. Therefore, you must be very specific in your searches. Using appropriate keywords and operators will help you refine your search.

Browsing first with your students probably helped them identify a list of appropriate keywords that they now have ready for their targeted searches. Now, to use search engines effectively, you must understand the language they use, called *Boolean operators*.

Boolean (and Other) Operators

Boolean logic uses a series of operators that are based in algebra. (For all of you math teachers out there, yes, it is just like the algebra you teach in your math class!)

Now is a perfect opportunity to launch into a brief mini-lesson on Boolean logic with your class, so the students can search more skillfully. According to Jamie McKenzie, it is imperative that students learn to use these operators in the context of their searches. McKenzie identifies effective searching as one of the key signs of progress that schools are becoming information-literate. In his book *How Teachers Learn Technology Best*, he describes searching in an information-literate school community like this: "Learners apply Boolean logic. They search with appropriate syntax. They employ powerful search strategies to carve through mountains of information" (1999, p. 61).

Explain to your students that using logical operators when conducting their searches will help them narrow the results found by online directories, search engines, and metasearch engines (which we'll discuss later)—giving them fewer and more accurate results to review. These operators are the language that the search tools use to interpret what the students are searching for, so their appropriate use enables students to search more efficiently.

Dr. Baron (2002) describes these operators, as reflected in the following table. The examples and results were added in order to clarify the importance of employing logic in your searching repertoire.

Boolean and Other Operators

Boolean Operators	Description	Example	Results
AND Plus sign (+)	Use *AND* between 2 words. Only the files with both words appear.	China AND Golden Age China + Golden Age	Narrows the search
OR	Use *OR* between 2 words. Only files containing one of the words will appear. This is useful for alternative spellings.	The Sung OR Song dynasties	Increases the number of results
NOT Minus sign (-)	Use *NOT* before a word to eliminate one meaning of the word or to exclude a word in the phrase.	The Song dynasty in china NOT song The Song dynasty in China - song	Narrows the search
Phrase Searching Operators	**Description**	**Example**	**Results**
Quotation Marks (" ")	Use quotation marks around a phrase to keeps the search terms together, creating a phrase.	"Tang and Song dynasty"	By creating a phrase, only the sites come up that have the exact phrase in the exact order as entered in your search engine. This narrows your results.
Truncation Operators	**Description**	**Example**	**Results**
Asterisk (*)	Use an asterisk at the end of the word to generate files with all variations of the word.	Snow* results in snowed, snowfall, snowball, snowy	Expands the number of results
Question Mark (?)	Use a question mark in place of a letter in a word, as a single "wildcard" letter.	s?ng results in sing, song, sung, sang	Expands the number of results

Have the students go back and enhance the keywords recorded in the notes section of their Cmap organizers with appropriate search operators. Remember that students need to be taught these skills in context!

To further develop your students' Boolean operators skills, distribute Handout I-4.

I-4 Boolean and Other Search Operators

Directions: Use this handout to create a list of keywords for a targeted online search. Follow the steps below to create your list.

Open up the notes section in your Cmap organizer. In the first column of the chart below, write the key terms you identified while browsing for your topic and subtopics in the online directories.

Use the second column to create searchable phrases from your key terms. A *searchable phrase* is a key term enriched with search operators.

For example, if your key terms are
- China
- golden age
- Tang dynasty
- Song dynasty

Your searchable phrases could be
- China + golden age
- "China's Golden age"
- Tang and Song dynasty
- S?ng dynasty + golden age

Try creating your own searchable phrases, using your key terms and search operators. This is a good time for you to experiment with the different operators to see which are the most beneficial for you.

Key Terms	Searchable Phrases
1.	
2.	
3.	
4.	
5.	

Once you have created your searchable phrases, you should include them in your Cmap organizer. Add the search operators to the key terms in the notes section.

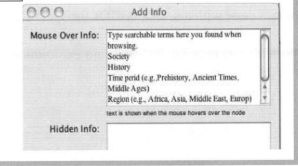

The Visible and Invisible Web

Your class is now ready to go on the World Wide Web to start your efficient targeted searches.

But before your class embarks on their virtual adventure on the Web, you should discuss where they should start their searching. It's an awfully big Web after all!

In a 10-minute mini-lesson, introduce these guiding questions to your students:

- What search engines are you going to use?
- Are you going to use the visible Web or the invisible Web?
- Are you going to use a metasearch engine?
- When should you use each of these different tools?

Have your students copy these questions in their learning journals. Explain to them that they will be exploring these questions over the next couple of weeks (or whatever your time line may be). Now you can work with your library media specialist to begin explaining to the students the difference between the visible and invisible Web.

The Information Constructivist knows that the *visible Web* is everything that can be found using search engines, online directories, and metasearch engines. "The visible Web is easy to define. It's made up of HTML Web pages that the search engines have chosen to include in their indexes. It's no more complicated than that" (Sherman & Price, 2001, p. 55).

The *invisible Web* (or deep Web) is everything that cannot be "seen" using the tools just mentioned. The invisible Web contains the files that those tools have trouble indexing, the files that are located in specialized databases.

An important note:

> Many invisible Web sites are made up of straightforward Web pages that search engines could easily crawl and add to their indexes, but do not—simply because the engines have decided against including them. This is a crucial point. Much of the invisible Web is hidden because search engines have deliberately chosen to exclude some types of content. We're not talking about unsavory "adult" sites or blatant spam sites. Quite the contrary! Many invisible Web sites are first-rate content sources. (Sherman & Price, 2001, p. 55)

To find information on the invisible Web, you must tell your students to go directly to the invisible Web or to a page with a search box for the specified databases they are seeking.

With all this in mind, let's start our exploration with the visible Web.

Producing Results on the Visible Web: Search Engines

Students type keywords into the search box of a search engine or an online directory, and click on "Search" or hit the Enter button on their keyboard. The search engine then looks for files in its indexed database that match those keywords.

Whatever the search engine finds that matches the students' keywords is listed on the results pages it returns. The search engine also indexes those Web pages, so they will quickly pop up when another user enters the same keywords in the search box.

Here are three effective search engines that you and your students should become familiar with when searching the visible Web:
• www.alltheweb.com
• www.google.com
• www.teoma.com

As your students become familiar with the unique features of each of these search engines, they can conduct more refined and targeted searches, with fewer and more accurate results. This allows them to spend less time searching through all the different links their searches provide and spend more time reading the information and constructing new ideas.

Set aside an entire class period to introduce your students to these three search engines. Allow time for them to conduct their own searches online and then reflect on their searches (Handout I-5, p. 48).

AlltheWeb

AlltheWeb is one of the few search engines that attempts to search both the visible and the invisible Web. It matches your students' search term(s) with the files on the visible Web and with multimedia files on the invisible Web.

AlltheWeb divides its home page into several different search sections: Web pages, news, pictures, FTP files, video files, and mp3 files. Students can select which tab they want for their search. AlltheWeb also has an Advanced Search page to help your students write more targeted searches. Students should read through the information on this page to learn the nuances of this search engine. (AlltheWeb also has a neat feature that allows you to select the language of the Web pages that you want to see.)

Searching with AlltheWeb

Students should type their keywords in the search box and then click on each of the tabs to find matching information of various file types. Or they can browse for information using the Fast Topics feature.

For example, if they are doing a search on President Clinton, they could type his name in the search box and select Search. On the first tab, they would see the Web pages that meet their search criteria. On the second tab, they would get news about former President Clinton.

If they continue clicking through all the different tabs they would see pictures, videos, MP3 files, and FTP files about President Clinton. Or they could use the Fast Topics directory that comes up as soon as they enter the search term on the home page.

Google

The anatomy of the Google™ search engine's Advanced Search page is so intricate that your students need to become familiar with its different features in order to use the Google™ search engine to its fullest potential.

On the opposite page is a snapshot of the Google™ search engine's Advanced Search page. This feature can be accessed by typing "www.google.com." On the home page, to the right of the search box, you will see the Advanced Search option. Students should become used to accessing this page and entering their key terms and phrases here.

When using the Advanced Search feature of the Google™ search engine, students don't need to include Boolean operators. Students should complete the boxes under "Find Results" in order to help narrow their results. The Google™ search engine will return Web pages containing the keywords entered. These pages are ranked in order by which company or individual paid the most (to be first on the list) and by which pages contain the most hyperlinks.

Searching with Google

To conduct a targeted search with the Google™ search engine, remember these pointers:

1. Type the most obvious and specific keywords first.

   General terms like "where" and "how" slow down the search process. The Google™ search engine will automatically omit these terms from most of your searches, so save time and leave them out!

2. The Google™ search engine recognizes + and – signs as operators when you are using its basic search features; however, it does not recognize the words AND and NOT. Do not use those words in your Google™ search: The Google™ search engine will omit them!

3. Put quotation marks around common phrases. That helps the Google™ search engine refine the matches you receive in your results.

Teoma

Teoma ranks its Web pages using a subject-specific method. This method ranks a Web site by the number of pages with the same subject, rather than on the site's popularity. This creates a more academic search engine because it returns results identified by subject area experts rather than those the general public finds important or interesting. The subject-specific directory delivers highly authoritative Web pages. Teoma's goal is to deliver high-quality Web pages, not just a high quantity of them.

Searching with Teoma

After you've entered your keyword(s), Teoma offers a tool to help you refine and focus the results of your search. On the left side of the page, it provides links to sites that experts recommend.

Distribute the Reflect on Search Engines handout on the next page (Handout I-5) to your students. Have them revisit each of the search engines introduced as they complete the handout.

Google™ Advanced Search

Find results	with **all** of the words		10 results ▾	Google Search
	with the **exact phrase**			
	with **at least one** of the words			
	without the words			

Language	Return pages written in	any language ▾
File Format	Only ▾ return results of the file format	any format ▾
Date	Return web pages updated in the	anytime ▾
Occurrences	Return results where my terms occur	anywhere in the page ▾
Domain	Only ▾ return results from the site or domain	
		e.g. google.com, .org More info
SafeSearch	⦿ No filtering ○ Filter using SafeSearch	

Page-Specific Search

Similar	Find pages similar to the page		Search
		e.g. www.google.com/help.html	
Links	Find pages that link to the page		Search

Topic-Specific Searches

Google Print - Search the full text of books
Google Scholar - Search scholarly papers

Apple Macintosh - Search for all things Mac
BSD Unix - Search web pages about the BSD operating system
Linux - Search all penguin-friendly pages
Microsoft - Search Microsoft-related pages

U.S. Government - Search all .gov and .mil sites
Universities - Search a specific school's website

I-5 Reflect on Search Engines

Directions: Use the World Wide Web and explore the different search engines that have been introduced to you.

Answer the reflection questions below to help you better understand the different search engines and how to use them.

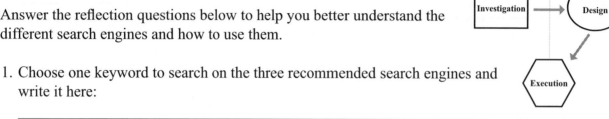

1. Choose one keyword to search on the three recommended search engines and write it here:

_____

2. In the chart below, write the top three results each search engine gave you for the keyword.

AlltheWeb	1. 2. 3.
Google	1. 2. 3.
Teoma	1. 2. 3.

4. How did these search engines provide you with different results?

_____
_____
_____

5. Were any of the results the same?

_____
_____
_____

6. Which search engine did you find the easiest to use?

_____

7. When would you use each search engine again?

_____
_____
_____

Metasearch Engines

Metasearch engines should be used when you want your query to be conducted on a number of different search engines at one time. The metasearch engine takes the keyword(s) you type in and searches multiple search engines. Then it returns the results from each of those search engines to you.

"Rather than crawling the Web and building its own index, a metsearch engine relies on the indexes created by other search engines. This allows you to quickly get results from more than one general purpose search engine" (Sherman & Price, 2001, p. 44).

Two of the more prevalent metasearch engines are MetaCrawler and Dogpile.

MetaCrawler.com

MetaCrawler uses innovative metasearch technology to search the Internet's top search engines—including Google, Yahoo! Search, MSN Search, Ask Jeeves, About, MIVA, and LookSmart.

MetaCrawler searches each of the search engines quickly and efficiently after you type your keyword(s) in its search box. MetaCrawler returns the results from each search engine, so you can access the results from the different search engines on MetaCrawler's home page—without having to go to each search engine individually.

Dogpile.com

Dogpile is a metasearch engine that uses "Arfie" the dog to fetch the results from the Internet's top search engines like Google, Yahoo! Search, MSN Search, Ask Jeeves, About, MIVA, and LookSmart.

It actually searches more than two dozen major search sites, including Usenet newsgroups, FTP sites for file downloads, newswires for current headlines, and business news from several sources. Unlike MetaCrawler, which post-processes the results using its own relevance algorithms, Dogpile returns the exact results from each engine with the utmost haste. Results are presented as each engine replies to the query. Dogpile searches three sites at a time. Results from each search engine are grouped together, with the descriptions provided by each site. At the bottom of the result is a button that continues your search with the next three search engines. (Sherman & Price, p. 45)

Have your students use the following handout (Handout I-6) to experiment with these and other popular metasearch engines.

I-6 Reflect on Metasearch Engines

Directions: Access any two of the four metasearch engines listed below and use the keyword you used in your search engine reflection handout (Handout I-5) to conduct a search on that same keyword using a metasearch engine.

Metasearch Engines

Dogpile: http://www.dogpile.com

MetaCrawler: http://www.metacrawler.com

Ixquick: http://www.ixquick.com

Ask Jeeves: http://askjeeves.com

Write the two metasearch engines you are accessing here:

1. _____

2. _____

In the table below, write the search engines that each of these metasearch engines accesses:

Metasearch Engine	Search Engines Accessed
1.	• • • • •
2.	• • • • •

Type in your keyword in each of the metasearch engines and describe below the results each metasearch engine retrieved.

_____
_____
_____
_____
_____
_____

Keane, *Internet-Based Student Research: Creating to Learn with a Step-by-Step Approach* © 2005.

Producing Results on the Invisible Web

The invisible Web consists of databases of information, images, and sound files that aren't indexed by the search engines on the visible Web. It includes "text pages, files, and other, often high-quality authoritative, information available via the World Wide Web that general-purpose search engines cannot (due to the technical limitations) or will not (due to the deliberate choice) add to their indexes of Web pages. The invisible Web is sometimes referred to as the 'Deep Web' or 'dark matter'" (Sherman & Price, 2001, p. 57).

Search engines cannot search databases, and they have trouble indexing Web pages that have URLs containing a percent sign (%). Search engines on the visible Web also have a hard time indexing sound and image files that have no text associated with them.

Other files that are part of the invisible Web are pages that the search engines have not yet identified and pages that have little or no HTML text in them.

Searching the Invisible Web

The invisible Web should be accessed for authoritative and finite searches. The invisible Web produces accurate and precise results, and the content is very focused.

For example, if you were searching for a bed and breakfast on Cape Cod in Massachusetts, you could use the invisible Web to access a directory of bed and breakfast listings. The invisible Web would provide you access to the bed and breakfast database created by the Massachusetts government.

Chris Sherman and Gary Price identify a number of topics that you and your students may want to search for on the invisible Web. Here are some examples of these topics:

Public Company Findings	Databases
Patents	Library Catalogs
Archived Material	Interactive Tools
Telephone Numbers	Authoritative Dictionaries
Company Financing Information and Directories	Historical Stock Quotes

The invisible Web looks like and is categorized like an online directory. In general, the home pages of the invisible Web databases and directories can be searched using three different techniques: category browsing, a quick search, or an advanced search.

Invisible Web Search Engines

Invisible Web Search Engine	URL Address
Academic Info	http://academicinfo.net
CompletePlanet	http://www.completeplanet.com

Each invisible search engine has its own unique ways in which it can be searched. You need to read through the Help menu to understand how to use each invisible Web search engine operates.

For example, CompletePlanet™ has three ways it can be searched. You can use the quick search or advanced search options on its home page, or you can use the Deep Query Manager to tap into subject-specific databases. You can access the Deep Query Manager by selecting the "To BrightPlanet" tab from the home page.

Use Handout I-7 Reflect on the Invisible Web, on the next page, to start exploring this new invisible world with your students.

Assessing Student Progress

Your students have learned a lot about researching online. It may be a good time to give them a review and evaluate their performance so far.

On page 54 is Handout I-8, which lists the top 10 online searching strategies. It is ready for you to reproduce and distribute to your students to help them as they conduct their research.

On page 55 is a checklist for you to use when assessing your students' progress in the research portion of their project. Remember, it can be helpful for students to have this information at the beginning of the lesson so they know what is expected of them. For that reason, the checklist is provided as a separate page that you can easily copy and distribute.

I-7 Reflect on the Invisible Web

Directions: Use the questions below to reflect on your journey on the invisible Web. These notes will help you when you use the invisible Web for your future research projects.

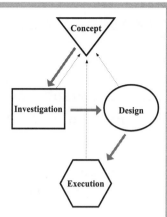

1. List two search engines you visited:

Invisible Web Search Engine	URL Address	Brief Description of the Page
1.		
2.		

2. How were the invisible search engines alike?

_____

_____

_____

_____

_____

_____

3. How were the invisible search engines different?

_____

_____

_____

_____

_____

_____

_____

_____

I-8 The Top 10 Online Searching Strategies

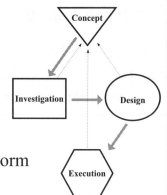

1. Use a graphic organizer like CmapTools to clarify your information challenge.

2. Use online directories to browse for your subject and brainstorm a list of keywords.

3. Decide if your research topic needs to be refined.

4. Become familiar with a few online directories, search engines, and metasearch engines that will be useful to you.

5. Read the Help tips provided by the search engines.

6. Keep the list of Boolean operators handy, so you can use them to write more targeted queries.

7. Take advantage of the different features the search engines offer.

8. Know when to use the visible Web and when to use the invisible Web.

9. Read through the titles and summaries of the matches in your search results before clicking on the links.

10. As you read through the titles and summaries, bookmark the Web pages that are relevant to your subject.

Research Checklist

Directions: Use the following checklist to make sure that
you are on track with your research.

_____ Thought about, brainstormed, discussed, and gathered information
about your topic in a prewriting exercise.

_____ Used a graphic organizer to clarify your information challenge.

_____ Browsed online directories to refine your subject matter.

_____ Demonstrated ability to conduct targeted online searches using Boolean
operators.

_____ Used the search engines' advanced search features.

_____ Used the visible Web and the invisible Web appropriately.

_____ Bookmarked relevant Web pages to help you with your research.

_____ Completed Handouts I-1 through I-7.

_____ Used class time wisely.

_____ Worked well with others in the classroom.

Authentication

> *How many versions of the truth are you looking for? Too often students accept information that looks authentic as the truth and this is one of the dangers of Web site information. Since ANYONE can publish on the Internet, learning how to validate information is an important skill.* – Alan November, www.novemberlearning.com

The World Wide Web provides a wealth of information to you and your students, but you need a process for evaluating the Web pages and authenticating their sources.

The No.1 guru in Web-site authentication is Alan November. Alan November breaks down the "Grammar of the Internet" into eight steps for you and your students to use. One of the activities on his Web site (www.novemberlearning.com) is an information-literacy quiz. Take the quiz with your students before beginning this lesson in class. You might want to photocopy the quiz and distribute it, or you can have your students take the quiz online. Don't worry. The next step in his breakdown of the Grammar of the Internet is to provide you with the answer key.

In this book, we will review two of Alan November's five techniques for evaluating a Web site and ensuring its authenticity. If you have more classroom time and want to teach your students all five of his techniques, you can access his site. You can find the information-literacy material by clicking on "Resources." The activities and other materials he makes available on his Web site will take one to two periods to cover in your classroom. It is an excellent site for both you and your students!

On the other hand, if you don't have an entire period to devote to authenticating Web pages or don't think your students will have the patience to run each Web site they want to use for their projects through all five tests, try the expedited authentication process described below:

1. Read the Uniform Resource Locator (URL) address.

   This is one of the most important skills you can teach your students. It is a quick and easy process, so most students are likely to use it.

2. Find out what other Web pages are hyperlinked to the page.

Reading the Uniform Resource Locator (URL)

A URL address, or Internet address, is similar to a regular mail address. It describes the location of a Web page.

URLs are very specific and some are even case-sensitive. The smallest typographical errors, like extra spaces or periods, can make it impossible to reach a site.

A URL address contains a series of network names separated by dots (.), slashes (/), and tildes (~). It usually begins with the name of the server or subnetwork and is followed by the domain name. As the following table from Dr. Baron's *Bud's Easy Research Paper Computer Manual* illustrates, different domain names signify different types of organizations.

Different Domain Names

Domain Name	Stands For	Domain Name	Stands For
.com	Commercial and business	**.edu**	Educational institutions
.gov	Government agencies	**.mil**	Military organizations
.net	Network resources	**.org**	Other organizations
.pro	Professionals such as doctors and lawyers	**.aero**	Air industry
.biz	General use	**.coop**	Business cooperatives
.info	General use	**.museum**	Museums
.name	Personal Web sites		

The URL address below is dissected to give you a better example of how to interpret a URL address on your own.

This URL example, from Alan November's Web site, is particularly interesting because it demonstrates to students the importance of authenticating their online source material. This Web site claims that the Holocaust never happened and that the information was written by a professor at Northwestern University. It would be a great lesson to have the students access the page and read it; then explain to them the dissection of the URL address.

This exercise can help students learn the importance of evaluating their source material and how they can determine if a Web site is an official page (e.g., supported by Northwestern University) or a personal page.

http://pubweb.northwestern.edu/~abutz/di/intro.html
     1   **2**   **3**   **4** **5** **6**

1. "pubweb" is a common term in a URL. It means public Web server. This is a clue that this a personal posting.

2. "northwestern.edu" is the domain name: "northwestern" stands for Northwestern University; "edu" stands for U.S. higher learning.

3. The "~" is a second clue that this a personal posting. A tilde represents a personal directory.

4. "abutz" following the tilde reveals that this a directory for Arthur Butz.

5. "di" refers to the subdirectory or folder.

6. "intro.html" means that this is the introductory page to the site.

Discovering What Web Pages Are Hyperlinked

A quick look at who has linked to a site might help you gain perspective about the quality of its information. A generated list of external links potentially gives you a range of thoughts or comments about any given Web page. – Alan November, www.novemberlearning.com

To find out what other Web pages have hyperlinked themselves to the subject Web page, you can use the "Link:" feature on Google and AltaVista.

1. Highlight the URL address of the Web page and copy it into Google's or AltaVista's search box.
2. Place your cursor in front of the URL address and type "link:"
3. Select "Search" or "Enter."

This type of search returns all of the Web pages that have linked themselves to the site in question. You should click a few links and see if any authoritative sites have linked themselves to the subject Web site.

3. Organization

Now you and your students have been researching for a few class days and have found lots of great information sources on the Internet. Your students have collected Web pages and other information that will help them with their projects. They have saved a lot of information in their Cmap visual diagrams. They have also printed out some Web pages. Some students may have neatly filed their materials in a folder, while others may have stuffed theirs in their lockers.

- What are the students going to do next?
- How are you going to help them sort through all of this information?
- How can you help them finish their projects in a timely fashion?

You need to help your students get organized—now.

This is an important step in the students' projects because the students will need to refer to the information they've gathered later, when they are putting together their projects (and their list of information sources).

This chapter will discuss some of the computer's many features that can help you and your students organize information.

The following pages are written to guide you through learning these new features, but they can also be used as handouts for your students.

It's up to you. Some teachers like to have the students sitting in rows and following along as they demonstrate bookmarking and creating "index cards"—while other teachers like to photocopy the pages for their students and ask them to figure it out on their own. It really depends on your teaching style and comfort level. This section should be flexible enough to work with whatever your style may be.

Coming Up Next:
- Bookmarking Web Sites
- Creating "Index Cards"

Investigation

Bookmarking Web Sites

Bookmarks are a personal list of Web sites that make it quick and easy to access your favorite places on the World Wide Web. A bookmark on the Web is just like a bookmark in a book. A bookmark in a book holds your page in the book while a bookmark on the Web holds your Web page on the Internet.

Bookmarks can be created using "Bookmarks" or "Favorites," depending on the Internet browser you are using. You can even create a virtual set of bookmarks online that can be remotely accessed from wherever you are.

Bookmarks are organized like file cabinets, divided into folders and subfolders to organize documents in their appropriate categories. Each folder is designated for a specific subject matter and should hold only the documents that pertain to that subject matter.

The Favorites or Bookmarks icon opens your collected Web pages and allows you to add, organize, and delete them.

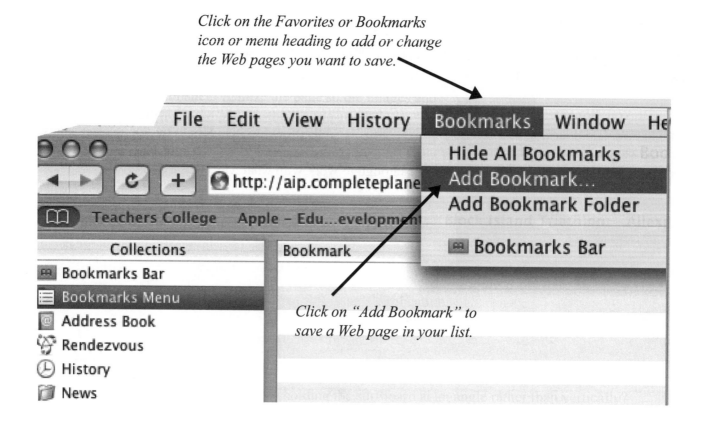

Click on the Favorites or Bookmarks icon or menu heading to add or change the Web pages you want to save.

Click on "Add Bookmark" to save a Web page in your list.

You may want to use an LCD projector.to show your students how to bookmark Web sites. You could also write down the following steps on your whiteboard or chalkboard. You could also show your students how to create folders to organize their bookmarks. Have them, as a class, click on the drop-down menu that says "Bookmarks" and then select "Add Bookmark Folder." They should name their folders based on the projects they are working on. Students can now add Web sites to their designated folders and keep their work more organized.

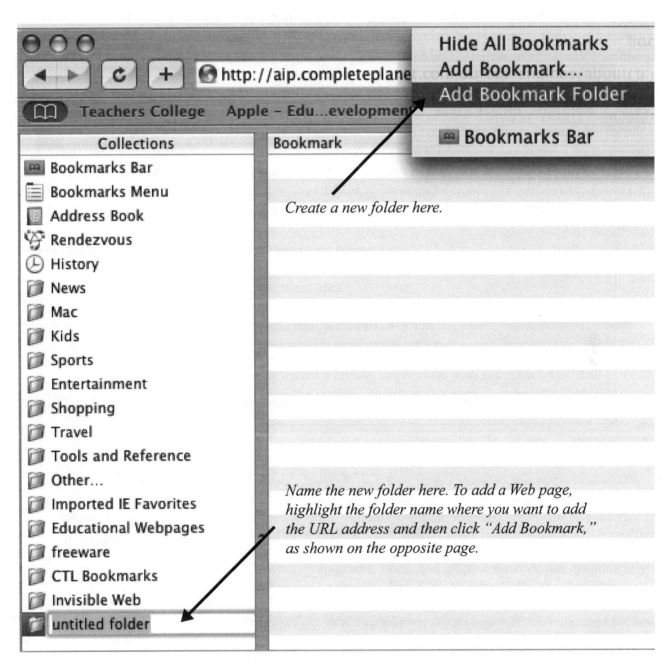

Create a new folder here.

Name the new folder here. To add a Web page, highlight the folder name where you want to add the URL address and then click "Add Bookmark," as shown on the opposite page.

You can delete a bookmark by selecting the bookmarked Web page and then pressing the Delete button. You can also organize your bookmarks into folders by dragging and dropping them into the appropriate folders.

Backflipping Web Sites

Backflip is the most convenient way to bookmark your sites so you can access them from any location that has Internet access. Your Backflip account can be quickly set up by accessing www.backflip.com. The Backflip home page has a place to set up your own free account. A Backflip icon can be dragged to your Web browser's menu page.

To add a Web page to your Backflip account, click on the Backflip shortcut on your top browser menu. You will be prompted to sign into your Backflip account so you can access the appropriate folder to store your Web page. To retrieve your Backflipped Web pages from a remote location, go to www.backflip.com and enter your username and password. This should give you access to the folders you added to Backflip, as well as to other people's public folders.

Creating "Index Cards"

To keep yourself organized, you should not only keep all of your Web pages bookmarked, but also create detailed "index cards" to track the Web pages you are going to use in your research. You can make these virtual index cards using Microsoft Word or Microsoft Excel. With these virtual index cards, you can collect all your research into one database, a great way to sort and organize information.

Jamie McKenzie discussed the idea of creating databases to store and track online research in his book *How Teachers Learn Technology Best*:

> The infotective collects the most important clues and files them in an organized manner that makes retrieval and synthesis easier at a later time. The infotective usually outgrows a word processor for note-taking and opts for a database that will support more powerful searching, sorting, and manipulating of data. (1999, p. 49)

Remember, McKenzie defines *infotectives* as people who make meaning in the Information Age. "They puzzle their way through piles of fragments—sorting, sifting, weighing, and arranging them until a picture emerges" (1999, p. 52).

An effective database can be created in Micrsosoft Word or Excel. Both programs will offer you a way to organize the information you find online and a way to put the information you read online into your own words. The following pages contain information about these two software programs, including detailed steps of how to create virtual index cards or databases to help you organize your research.

Constructing Microsoft Word Databases

1. Choose "Insert Table" from the "Table" drop-down menu on the top toolbar.

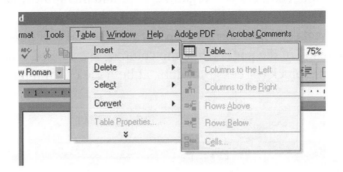

2. You will be prompted to select how many rows and columns you want in your table. (Don't worry. You can always go back and add or delete rows and columns later.)

3. You should set up the table like a research index card. You will use this "index card" table to take notes about the Web pages you have bookmarked. See the example below.

4. Once you create your first table, you may want to highlight it, and copy and paste it a few times, so you have an index card for each of the Web pages you are using in your project.

Sample Research Index Card

Title of the Article	
Author	
Source (URL)	
Quick Dissection of URL Address	
3 Hyperlinked Sites	
Last Time the Page Was Updated	
Copyright Info	
Direct Quotes	
General Overview of the Web Page	

Microsoft Excel

Large research projects require larger databases to store all the information that you collect. Microsoft Excel is a software program that can help you organize, sort, and manipulate large quantities of data.

Excel is set up as a spreadsheet (grid), in horizontal rows and vertical columns. The rows are labeled with numbers down the left side of the page, while the columns are labeled with letters across the top of the page. To identify a specific block (or *cell*), you look at both the column letter and the row number (e.g., B4).

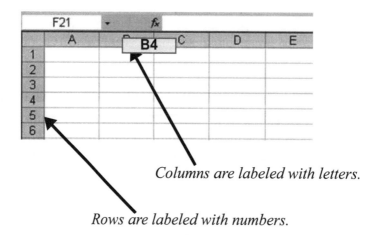

Columns are labeled with letters.

Rows are labeled with numbers.

To move from cell to cell within an Excel spreadsheet, you can use the Tab or arrow buttons on your keyboard. You can also point and click with your mouse to select a specific cell.

Each Excel file (or *workbook*) that you create can contain multiple pages (or *sheets*), which can help you organize your information. To move from one sheet to another, simply click on the sheet's tab at the bottom of your screen

You can see all the sheets in your workbook at the bottom of your screen. You can name these sheets by double-clicking on the name (e.g., "Sheet1") and typing the new name.

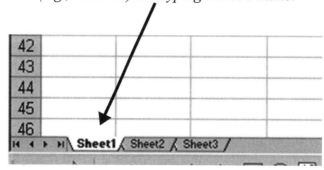

As you begin to use your Excel database and add information to it, you are going to need to resize and format your cells.

You can resize a column or row of cells by moving your mouse pointer near the appropriate letter or number identifier. When the arrow turns into a skinny cross, you can drag (with your left mouse button pressed) to make the column or row larger or smaller.

If you want to resize multiple columns or rows, you can use the "Format Cells" drop-down menu from the toolbar.

In addition to the size of columns and rows, the "Format Cells" menu allows you to change the alignment of text within cells (e.g., left, center, right), cell borders and shading, and font type and size.

You can also choose to have the text wrap or shrink to fit within the cells by checking the appropriate box under "Text Control" on the "Alignment" tab.

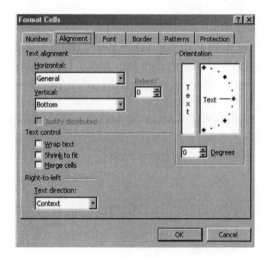

The Excel sheets are already set up as tables, like the one you created using Microsoft Word, so setting up index cards in Excel is very easy. Just follow the steps on the following pages.

Constructing Microsoft Excel Databases

1. Add category headings to a blank worksheet. Begin by typing the word *Title* in cell A1. Type the rest of the categories across Row 1, one category in each cell (see p. 63 for suggested categories).

2. Under the appropriate category headings, type in the information you want the database to track. You will have one row for each "index card."

3. Resize and reformat the columns and rows to make viewing the data easier. Use your mouse to move the borders or use the more detailed "Format" menu, as described earlier.

4. Quickly sort your data using the A/Z icon in the toolbar. Click anywhere in the column that you want to sort by (e.g., author) and then click the A/Z icon. All your index cards will be sorted in ascending alphabetical order by the author names.

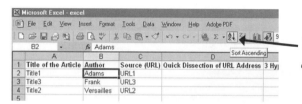

The A/Z icon sorts data in ascending alphabetical order.

5. To sort your data based on more than one column of data (for example: by date, then by author), use the "Data" menu and click on "Sort." You can choose up to three columns of data to use as sorting criteria.

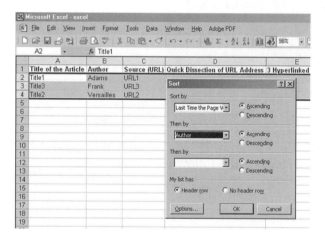

6. To make sifting through and understanding your data even easier, you can add filters to your columns. Go to the "Sort" menu and click on "Filter" and "Autofilter." You will then be able to select criteria in each column to display only the records that match those criteria. For example, you can display only those sources that were updated after a certain date and written by a particular author.

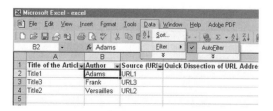

Adding Information to Your Index Cards

1. Your Web browser and database document must be opened simultaneously, with the database window minimized and the Web browser window maximized. Toggling between the two programs allows you to quickly cut and paste information from Web pages into your database.

2. Highlight the portion of the Web page (e.g., the URL, text for direct quotes) that you want to include in your database. Use the Ctrl+C command on the PC (the Apple+C on the Mac) to copy the information. Then paste it into your Word or Excel database. (The paste command on the PC is Ctrl+V and on the Mac is Apple+V.)

3. Take a few minutes to write a quick summary of the online information in the "my own words" category of your database.

4 Reread the information challenge in your original research diagram to determine if the information you have collected addresses your information challenge.

5. As you reread your outline and your notes, add final notes and comments to your database.

Assessing Student Progress

Your students are finally at the end of the Investigation phase of their projects. It is now time to formally evaluate their performance.

Use Handout I-9 Reflect on the Investigation Section, on the next two pages, with your students as a review of this section.

On pages 70 and 71 are a checklist and rubric for you to use when assessing students' progress in this phase. This would be a good time to work with the library media specialist in assessing your students progress.

Remember, it can be helpful for students to have this information at the beginning of the lesson so they know what is expected of them. For that reason, the checklist and rubric are provided as separate pages that you can easily copy and distribute.

I-9 *Reflect on the Investigation Section*

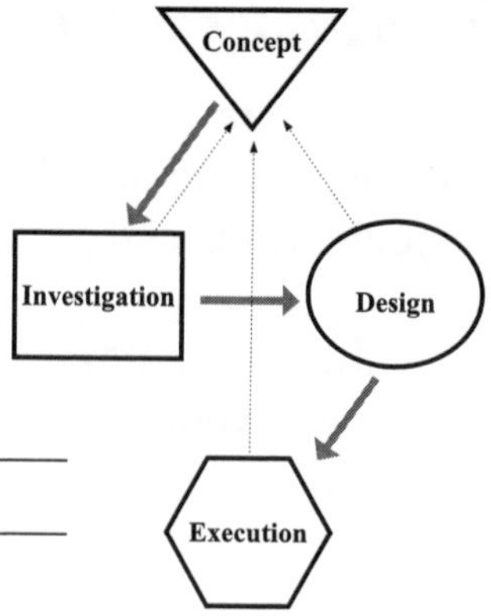

Directions: Answer the questions below.

1. What is the first step in the online research process?

_____

_____

2. What do you use the invisible Web for?

_____

_____

_____

_____

3. What are two ways of validating your online sources?

_____

_____

_____

4. For big research projects, what methods are available to use for organizing your research information?

_____

_____

_____

_____

5. Write down as many steps of the online research process as you can remember.

_____

_____

_____

_____

_____

_____

_____

_____

_____

_____

I-9 Reflect on the Investigation Section (cont.)

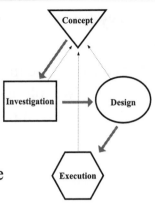

The Investigation Phase: A Summary Review

1. Restate your information challenge in a graphical organizer. (CmapTools is a great software program to help you visualize your concepts.)

2. Browse through online directories to gather a list of key terms. Create searchable phrases with the key terms and Boolean operators. Reread your information challenge and add any related subtopics that you found while browsing through the online directories.

3. Decide where you should search for your subject: that is, on the visible Web or the invisible Web.

4. Search online.

5. Validate the online sources you find by dissecting URL addresses and by investigating what other Web pages are linked to the pages you've found.

6. Record the information you found online by bookmarking the Web pages.

7. Create a database where you can organize your notes. Review your notes and begin developing an outline of ideas for your project.

Savvy Investigation Checklist

Directions: Use the following checklist to make sure you have thoroughly explored the online strategies we've discussed and used them to complete the Investigation phase of your project.

_____ Took the information-literacy quiz on Alan November's Web site.

_____ Viewed the Web site created by Arthur Butz and understand why it is so important to dissect an Uniform Resource Locator address.

_____ Used Dr. Baron's domain names chart as a reference when you dissected the Web pages you are using for your research.

_____ Used Altavista's "link:" tool to find out who linked to the online sources you've located for your project.

_____ Sorted and sifted back through the Web pages collected during the first half of the research to validate URL addresses and to determine whether or not other scholarly and academic online resources are hyperlinked to them. In other words, you _analyzed_ the material.

_____ Bookmarked and backflipped valuable Web sites.

_____ Created index cards in Word or Excel to organize your research.

_____ Thoroughly completed index cards, to have a valuable tool when you start to create your knowledge entity.

_____ Used Handout I-9 to reflect on your research.

_____ Found a minimum of five valid Web pages that can be used for your project.

Rubric: Investigation Phase

The following rubric will be used to evaluate your performance in this phase of your project.

Investigation Rubric

	Not Yet	*Okay*	*Excellent*
Prewriting	You spent little or no time engaged in prewriting exercises.	You spent some time engaged in prewriting exercises, but did not thoroughly explore the topic.	You thoroughly explored the topic during prewriting activities. You brought up many valid questions and ideas during this time.
Browsing Online Directories	You spent little or no time browsing online directories to refine your subject.	You spent some time using online directories to refine your subject.	You used online directories to refine your topic and to gather more information about it. You added this information to your graphic organizer.
Using the Visible and Invisible Web and Search Engines	You performed a quick search using only one search engine.	You worked in both the visible and invisible Web, but didn't understand when to use one versus the other.	You conducted targeted searches in the visible and invisible Web. You had a clear understanding of which search engine to use and why.
Classroom Activities and Handouts	You did only a few of the classroom activities and handouts.	You did half of the classroom activities and handouts.	You were thoroughly engaged in the class and completed all of the handouts and reflection activities.
Bookmarking Web Pages	You bookmarked Web pages without analyzing the material.	You bookmarked Web pages and analyzed some of the material.	You thoroughly analyzed the Web pages before bookmarking them.
Validating Web Pages	You didn't evaluate any of the Web pages for authenticity.	You evaluated a few of the Web pages for authenticity.	You thoroughly evaluated the Web pages for authenticity. You dissected the URL addresses and checked who had hyperlinked to them.
Organizing Research	You made no attempt to organize your research.	You organized some of your research.	You made virtual index cards in an Excel database and used it to organize all of your research and to validate your data.

Works Cited

Baron, A. (2002). *Bud's easy research paper computer manual* (4th ed.). New York: Lawrence House Publishers.

McKenzie, J. (1997, October.). A picture is worth a thousand words: Graphical organizers as thinking technology. *From Now On.* Retrieved November 11, 2005, from http://www.fno.org/oct97/picture.html.

McKenzie, J. (1999). *How teachers learn technology best.* Bellingham, WA: FNO Press.

November, A. (1998, September). Teaching Zack to think. *High School Principal Magazine.* Retrieved August 2, 2005, from http://www.novemberlearning.com.

Sebranek, P., Kemper, D., & Meyer, V. (1999). *Write source 2000: A guide to writing, thinking, and learning.* Wilmington, MA: Great Source Education Group.

Sherman, C., & Price, G. (2001). *The invisible Web: Uncovering information sources search engines can't see.* Medford, NJ: CyberAge Books.

The Visual Architect

What? A visual architect? What's that?

What do you normally think of when someone uses the term *architect*? You probably think of houses, office buildings, bridges. Well, before any structure is built, someone has to design it—to create a blueprint showing all the features that will make the structure succeed in its goal.

The same idea applies to your students. They must carefully design their projects before they can start building them.

Jamie McKenzie refers to this stage as "envisioning." He explains:

> One type of thought involves conjuring. Identifying possibilities and exploring the unthinkable. How could things be changed or made better?

> The students conceive, conjecture, fancy, imagine, project, and visualize. Envisioning lifts the product and outcome of the thinking beyond past practice and old thinking. The thinker leaps out of the box of everyday, ho-hum thinking. Of course, grazing the Internet lends itself especially well to the encouragement of such flights of fancy. The Net provides excursions, journeys, safaris, sallies, and treks. Envisioning is the source of originality. It provides the energy for change. Cognitive dissonance. (McKenzie, 1999, p. 53)

After your students have finished their research in the Investigation phase, you need to include time in the curriculum to have them envision the possibilities, to create something new, to stew about their project choices, and to delve into the world of architecture. They need to grapple with the idea that they will be creating something new, that a new knowledge entity is being born.

A visual architect, then, chooses the type of media that works best for a project and then designs and produces a powerful communication tool.

This section describes several project options for your students to choose from and some overall principles that can help make these projects successful. It contains valuable information that will help students create blueprints of their projects.

This step in the CIDE process is imperative. It is where students need to take the time to synthesize their research and envision the possibilities—before they begin to create and move into the Execution phase.

Coming Up Next:
- Project Choices
- Global Design Principles
- Blueprint Time

Design

4. Project Choices

So how are you and your students going to show off their research and their new understanding about the topic? There are so many multimedia choices. How do your students pick the best one for their projects?

Embarking on project-based multimedia learning with your students opens all types of doors for them as learners. In their 2002 book, *Increasing Student Learning through Multimedia Projects*, Michael Simkins, Karen Cole, Fern Tavalin, and Barbara Means talk about this approach to learning:

> Project-based multimedia learning is a method of teaching in which students acquire new knowledge and skills in the course of designing, planning, and producing a multimedia product. Your students' multimedia products will be technology-based presentations, such as a computerized slide show, a Web site or a video. These presentations will include evidence that your students have mastered key concepts and processes you need to teach and will be a source of great pride for them and for you. (p. 2)

The information in this book lends itself to the following types of multimedia projects:
- A printed publication, like a research paper or brochure
- A PowerPoint presentation
- A slide show of photographs
- A movie production

So which type of knowledge entity should you and your students create?

Each student in your classroom will be drawn to a different type—one in which his or her unique intelligences can be fostered. Try to be flexible to account for those differences.

Carefully explain to students that many types of knowledge entities could reveal their own unique understandings, but some will work better than others, depending on factors like these:
- Their subject matter
- How broad or focused their research is
- Their purpose in presenting the information
- Who their audience is

This chapter will help you and your students pick the best medium for their projects, so they can start putting their ideas into action.

Coming Up Next:
- The Publisher
- The Presenter
- The Photographer
- The Producer
- Choosing the Right Medium

Design

So what options do you and your students have? First, turn on the computer and see what applications are available. You probably have a word processing program and a spreadsheet program. With these, you can produce text, figures, charts, graphs, and even some pictures.

If your school uses PCs or Macs, it is very likely that they have the entire Microsoft Office Suite for Educators installed on them. This software package includes Microsoft Word, Microsoft Excel, and Microsoft PowerPoint. With these programs, you can produce presentations, sophisticated graphs, text, charts, and some very basic pictures. Macintosh computers come loaded with the iLife suite. With this package, you have access to iTunes, iPhoto, and iMovie. Using these programs you can create playlists of your favorite songs, slide shows of your favorite pictures, and even video clips of your best footage.

> **Teacher Tip:** Finding out what software applications are available *in the beginning* can save you a lot of grief later on.

The bottom line? Be realistic. If you don't have a video camera, then you are probably not going to produce a movie. If you don't have a camera, then your students aren't going to be able to take pictures of their own; they will have to download them from the Internet. If your students do download pictures, it is a good time to discuss copyright laws and permissions with them.

In the next section, read about the different possibilities your students' projects can take. Students can learn to put on four different hats: the hats of the publisher, the presenter, the photographer, and the producer.

The Publisher

The publisher must present written words (text), often with other types of media, including photography, in a finished product. A good publisher knows his readers and how they react to certain layouts and ideas. The publisher's work covers a wide variety of printed materials, among them the research paper, the newsletter, and the magazine cover.

The Research Paper

Of all the media types, you and your students are probably the most familiar with the research paper. A research paper can cover broad or narrow topics and is an excellent way to combine research from multiple sources. "All ideas borrowed from different sources must be credited to the original writer or speaker. Most research papers are at least three pages in length and may include a title page, an outline, the actual essay, and a Works Cited page (bibliography)" (Sebranek et al., 1999, p. 223).

Students writing a more sophisticated research paper also include their unique conclusions about the research. Research papers of the past didn't include photos or artwork, but today, you and your students may be able to enhance their text with pictures. Don't forget pictures or artwork included in the text must be incorporated in your students' Works Cited list.

The Newsletter

A newsletter usually contains articles, editorials, images, and the publisher's mission statement and contact information—all within a stylized format that includes the publisher's logo. A good newsletter is informative and is also fun to browse and read. Students should balance information-heavy articles with lighter material, such as fun facts, word games, and graphics. Including a variety of activities allows them to connect with the varied interests of their audiences.

Ideal Uses: Newsletters can be an excellent medium for combining articles that all discuss the same general theme or subject, but are written by different authors. Newsletters are especially useful when doing group work. Group members can split the responsibilities for the various parts, such as articles, features, interviews, and photo essays.

The Magazine Cover

The cover of a magazine is the first impression potential readers get, so it must convince them to browse the magazine. The cover should contain captivating lead articles and a glimpse of other features within the magazine. Most importantly, the cover usually has a large attention-getting and thought-provoking picture—something that can be noticed from a distance.

Magazine covers are a good medium if your students like art or have a memorable image or piece of artwork to use. Remember, the image must not only engage the viewer but also provide insight into the material covered within the magazine. Cover pages also need to have teasers that highlight features or themes, to encourage viewers to read the remainder of the publication.

Caution: Students should be careful about choosing magazine covers for their projects. There is limited space for text on a cover; therefore, if the student has a lot of information that needs explaining, a magazine cover is not the right medium. If a student still wants to choose a cover project, you may want to consider requiring a piece of writing to accompany the magazine cover.

The Presenter

The presenter delivers a main idea to a live audience. She usually has a prepared speech complemented by one or more types of multisensory media, such as handouts, slide shows, illustrations on white boards or flip charts, audio clips, video clips, animations, models, artwork, or 3-D objects. These multimedia objects simultaneously highlight the most significant points of the speaker's presentation and spark the audience's interest. Although the presenter does the majority—and sometimes all—of the talking, a good presentation is interactive in some way. A powerful presenter uses interesting information and multimedia tools to involve the audience members and encourage their participation.

The Presentation

A presentation is a powerful way to share information with an audience if the presenter has content that is enhanced by explanations and prompts. The immediate and interactive nature of the presentation allows for questions and answers; therefore, it's a great medium for teaching new subject matter. The presentation also works well if you or your students want to use multiple forms of media to enhance the minimal amount of text included in the presentation.

> At least 90 percent of my slides have no words on them at all. Instead they have full-screen photographic images. All the words we've become accustomed to copying furiously from the overhead transparency or PowerPoint slide are in my handout or posted on my Web site.

What's left are the really important parts of the presentation: the personal stories, the shared experience, the interaction, and all the emotion conveyed in the images that capture the essence of what I'm most passionate about communicating. (Burmark, 2002, p. 64)

Students who give presentations need to be able to stand in front of the class and talk about their topics. While presentations are good for teaching and sharing verbal explanations of subject matter, they are not good for sharing long written works. The majority of the "text" in a presentation is spoken, not written.

In a classroom setting it is imperative that you explain to your students that a little text does not mean a little content. David Thornburg gave his students' presentations two grades: 1–10 points for technique and 1–10 points for content. Their final grade was determined by multiplying those two grades (Burmark, 2002, p. 62).

The Creating to Learn philosophy grades students on these three criteria:
• their understanding of the concept,
• the thoroughness of their investigation, and
• the execution of the presentation.

These critical factors help your students put together a successful presentation.

The Photographer

A picture is a great way to share an experience, a moment in time, or a place with someone. The appropriate photograph can enhance the subject matter of a project and personalize the work. Sometimes photographers take so many good pictures that they use them by themselves to create a knowledge entity. Two knowledge entities that depend heavily on the effective use of photographs are photo essays and slide shows.

> As you and your students select or create images for your multimedia project, take some time to look at pictures that you consider appealing. Because the subject matter is compelling, you become involved. The technical quality is probably high, too. Think about composition. Images that place the subject matter dead center are static, so place the main subject a little off-center. (Simkins et al., 2002, p. 14)

The Photo Essay

The photo essay is good when you want your students to tell a story with pictures. With an assortment of vivid photos, you and your students can share a moment in time or capture a human emotion. The photos must be able to communicate feeling on their own, without words. Students may add captions and background information to share additional information about a historical event, a moment in time, or any other type of story—but the majority of the communication will be through the photos.

Caution: Photo essays are not a good choice if the topic is better conveyed through action or movement. Photo essays are also not a good choice if students' pictures are not compelling.

The Slide Show

The slide show is similar to the photo essay in that it is good for a collection of pictures that share a story, a mood, or a moment in time. The slide show, however, usually has less text than a photo essay. Often, a slide show will have a verbal introduction and then be accompanied by music, ending with a brief verbal conclusion. The timing of a slide show is critical. The pace shouldn't be too slow, providing just enough time to appreciate each picture.

Caution: Slide shows are not a good choice if the photos need explanation. The pictures should speak for themselves, needing no more than a few captions.

The Producer

The producer creates movies! He uses scripts, film, actors, actresses, still pictures, music, and creative angle shots to put together productions. The producer is artistic, using his creativity to combine different media types to share his ideas, stories, and interests with an audience.

Producing requires an in-depth understanding of the topic. Your students must choose the type of production that best helps them share their unique understandings and stories. "Video clips are used in multimedia to convey pieces of information or ideas. In one project on Newton's laws of motion, students mixed text and diagrams about science content with video clips to demonstrate concepts like inertia" (Simkins et al., 2002, p. 23).

Three of the most typical production types used in the classroom setting are documentaries, video stories, and commercials.

The Documentary

The documentary is like a research paper in motion. It shares a wealth of research and expert opinion— when done correctly. A documentary mixes multiple sources such as interviews, motion pictures, still pictures, art, graphs, and music. The documentary is great for uncovering facts and presenting both sides of a situation or event. Subjects or historical events can be covered in detail with this type of production.

Caution: Documentaries are not a good choice if the subject isn't somewhat controversial or thought-provoking. Students should not choose a documentary if their subject is very narrow or is fictional.

Video Story

A video story is a fictional story. It starts with an introduction, and it has a climax and a resolution. This is a good way to teach students the different parts of a fictional storyboard in an English class. This type of production is also good for subjects that allow for creativity and aren't too in-depth or too broad. A video story can be used to demonstrate students' understandings or interpretation of a scene, book, or historical event. (Reenactments can be fun!) Remember video stories must have characters and a plot.

Caution: A video story is not a good choice if the student's subject doesn't have interesting characters and a good plot. Also, a video story may not be a good choice if the students have a particular objective with their subject matter.

The Commercial

The commercial is a great way to get your students to start learning about persuasion. Have your students choose a particular side of a topic to promote.

Commercials hit a subject quickly and dramatically. They also motivate people to take action. Therefore, commercials work well with very narrow topics that can generate strong opinions.

Caution: A commercial is not a good choice for an in-depth look at a subject. It is also not a good choice if your students need to take an objective standpoint and want to leave the audience with room to consider other viewpoints.

Choosing the Right Medium

1. Copy and distribute Handout D-1, on the opposite page, to your students.
2. Have your students complete the handout to get a better idea about what type of knowledge entity they should develop.
3. After they complete the handout, have them share their answers with a study partner in class.
4. Then copy and distribute the table on page 84. Have the students read it silently, with a partner, or as a class.
5. After reading through a summary table of the knowledge entities, have the students each circle the one that suits their own unique talents—if your objective is flexible.

> *Teacher Tip:* Depending on your objective, you may want all your students to do the same project. In this case, assign the class the knowledge entity that best suits the needs of your students and the availability of technology and software in your school.

Assessing Student Progress

Your students have learned a lot about different types of projects. This is a good time to check in with them and evaluate their project choices. On page 85 is a checklist for you to use.

Remember, it can be helpful for students to have this information at the beginning of the lesson so they know what is expected of them. For that reason, the checklist is provided as a separate page that you can easily copy and distribute.

D-1 Choosing the Right Medium

Directions: Before you decide what medium you think works best with your project, complete this worksheet to organize your thoughts.

1. State your project's concept, in your own words.

_____
_____
_____

2. What type of media did you find when you were researching your topic?

_____
_____

3. List three actions that you are good at—such as writing, taking pictures, or making speeches.

_____
_____
_____

4. Do you have pictures related to your topic? Can you get some? _____

5. Do you have access to a video camera? _____

6. Do you know of other publications, presentations, slide shows, photo essays, or movie productions about your topic?

_____
_____
_____

7. Write down three designs your concept can take. Ask the opinion of your learning partner or your teacher.

_____
_____
_____

D-1a Choosing the Right Medium: Reference Guide

The table below summarizes the different forms your knowledge entity can take.
Use it as a quick reference guide when deciding on your design.

Design	Good for projects with...	Primary media	Depth	Choose if you like...	Classroom examples
The Publisher					
Research Paper	Research from multiple sources; your unique conclusions about research	Text	In-depth or brief	Writing	A research paper on geocentric vs. heliocentric solar systems
Newsletter	Several separate parts addressing one theme: articles, features, interviews, photo essays	Text, photos	Brief	Working in groups; writing articles; finding vivid pictures	A newsletter from the 1920s, with articles about flappers, the jazz age, prohibition, and morality
Cover Page	Creative, memorable images or artwork; teasers, power words	Short text, photos	Very brief	Taking captivating photos; using power words to entice readers	A magazine cover about foods that prevent cancer
The Presenter					
Presentation	Content that would be enhanced by prompts and explanations, interactive teaching, Q&A	Short text, photos	Brief written, but detailed verbal	Speaking in front of others; explaining your ideas and knowledge	A presentation describing the difference between acceleration and velocity
The Photographer					
Photo Essay	Your artistic, interpretive statement about an emotionally charged issue	Photos, captions	Brief or in-depth	Taking vivid pictures	A photo essay showing one view of the Vietnam war
Slide Show	A collection of pictures that show a story, mood, or moment in time, without needing text	Photos, music	Brief	Coordinating the tone of pictures and music	A slide show of the genocide that occurred in Cambodia under the Khmer Rouge's regime
The Producer					
Documentary	Detailed descriptions of an issue or historical event, using multiple sources and media	Film, photos, music	In-depth	Shooting film; researching; presenting thought-provoking arguments	A documentary about Stalin, Hitler, and Mao, and the atrocities committed under their rule. Ask the audience to decide which was the most violent ruler.
Video Story	Subjects that allow you to be creative	Video	Brief	Acting; writing plots and character sketches; creating effective scenes	A reenactment from a scene in the novel *The House on Mango Street* by Sandra Cisneros
Commercial	Controversial topics, when trying to motivate people to action	Video	Brief	Calling people to action; making lasting impressions	A commercial making a case for drilling for oil in Alaska. (Another student can make a commercial with the opposite view.)

Project Choices Checklist

Directions: Use the following checklist to make sure you have taken appropriate steps to choose your project wisely.

```
        Concept
   Investigation → Design
          Execution
```

_____ Considered what type of knowledge entity would be appropriate for your subject matter.

_____ Evaluted the various aspects of the different types of projects in terms of what may work best for your purpose and with your time and technology limitations.

_____ Worked with a learning partner to discuss ideas for your knowledge entity.

_____ Completed Handout D-1, to narrow the choices for the right medium for your knowledge entity, and then discussed it with a learning partner.

5. Global Design Principles

Good design principles are a necessity when creating any type of communication. The implementation of design principles ensures that students' information is laid out in an appealing, logical, and cohesive manner.

Using Handout D-2, Introduction to Design, on the next page, introduce your students to the three most important elements of design briefly outlined below.

Organization

The major components of any type of communication project need to be arranged in a way that engages the audience.

Visual Expression

All nonverbal components (such as photographs, drawings, diagrams, and lines) need to work together to establish the tone of a project. Visual aspects like color, contrast, and balance play an important role in establishing the overall tone.

Written Text

The words need to be carefully chosen and appropriately formatted—into headings and captions. Tone, structure, and style are key.

Coming Up Next:
- Effective Organization
- Appropriate Visual Expression
- Powerful Text Messages
- Sketching Initial Ideas

Design

D-2 Introduction to Design

Directions: Look at this magazine cover, and then answer the following questions:

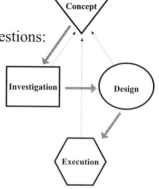

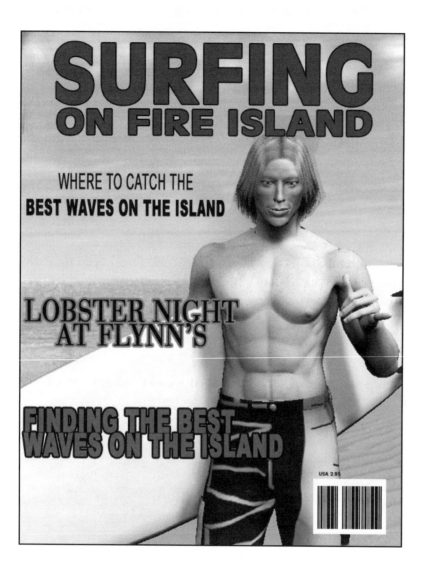

1. Which words did you see first? _____

   • What size are the letters?_____

2. Why do you think the boy is holding a surfboard diagonally across the page?_____
   _____

   • Why do you think the photographer didn't have the boy holding the surfboard straight up ?
   _____
   _____

Effective Organization

Everyone knows the importance of organizing content when writing a research paper, but few people are aware of its importance when creating a more visual publication.

> "Basically, a graphic designer's job is to be a translator, to put information into a visual form that gives people a better understanding of the content." – Wendy Richmond
>
> From *Designing for Communication: The Key to Successful Desktop Publishing*, by T. McCain, 1992, divider between pp. 30–31.

Visual organization is vital because the human eye follows a predictable pattern when initially scanning a page. The major components should grab and hold the audience's attention. A well-designed project gives the audience members enough information to engage them without confusing or overloading their senses.

In order for you and your students to organize material well, you need to understand a few principles of design. These principles will help you in laying out a page that takes full advantage of a reader's natural eye patterns:

• The "visual center"

• Natural page-scanning patterns

• "Hot areas" of a page

The Visual Center

The *visual center* of a page is the reader's initial point of engagement with the page. "Research has determined that when a reader encounters a new page, whether the page is tall or turned on its side, the eyes naturally gravitate to the left of the page along the golden mean line. Amazingly, the spot where the eyes go first is at the intersection of the two golden mean lines" (McCain, 1992, pp. 44–45). This is the visual center of the page, the first spot that the reader's eye is drawn to, and it is where the reader spends the most amount of his time when viewing the page. To communicate quickly and effectively, the publisher and presenter use this prime location on a page or slide wisely, placing high-impact images and headings there.

Distribute Handout D-3 to your students. Have them complete the handout quietly at their seats or in partners. Go over the handouts after a couple of minutes. Make sure the students understand the importance of the visual center of the page and how strategic it is to their designs.

The visual center of a page can be found using publishing standards that have been understood since the time of the ancient Greeks.

The ancient Greeks first defined the term *golden mean*, which divides a line (or page or slide) into two unequal parts, one being more prominent than the other. A page has both a horizontal and a vertical golden mean; the intersection of those lines is the visual center.

D-3 Location, Location, Location!

Directions: Look at this magazine cover, and then answer the following questions:

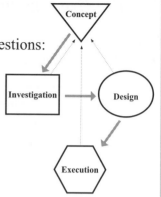

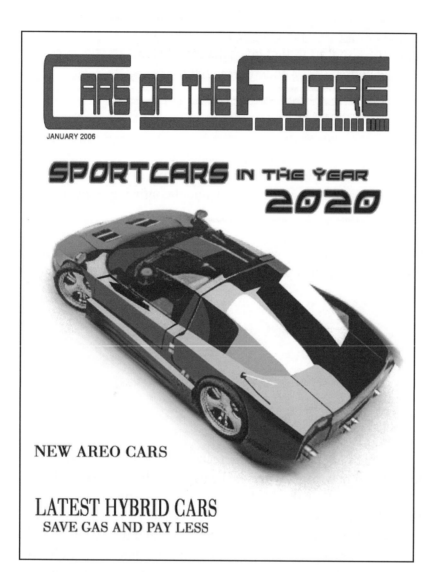

1. Where did you look first?_____

2. What effect do you think the placement of the image had on your view of the magazine's title?

_____

3. What is the name of the featured article in this issue of the magazine? _____

_____

• Where is the feature article's title placed? _____

• Why do you think it is placed there?_____

_____

To calculate the horizontal golden mean, divide the length of a page by 1.6. So, for a standard 8½" x 11" page, divide 11 by 1.6, and get 6.88, or approximately 7". The horizontal mean is approximately 7" up from the bottom edge of the page.

To calculate the vertical golden mean, divide the width of a page by 1.6. So, for an 8½" x 11" page, divide 8½ by 1.6, and get 5.31, or approximately 5½". The vertical mean is approximately 5½" from the right side of the page.

Where these two lines intersect is the visual center of the page.

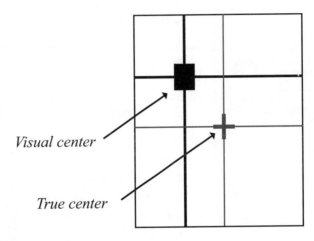

Visual center

True center

The Reader's Natural Scanning Pattern

When a reader encounters a page that has a variety of items, such as headlines, blocks of text, tables, graphs, photographs, and captions, the reader automatically scans the page to decide whether or not it is worth reading.

This initial scan begins with the visual center of the page and then sweeps through the page in a "Z" pattern. This illustration was created using Ted McCain's book *Designing for Communication: The Key to Successful Desktop Publishing*. In this book, McCain describes the way in which designers capitalize on this natural scanning behavior when they put their pages together:

"The items on the page are arranged to form a Z-pattern that the eye can easily follow. Because it is so easy for the reader to follow this pattern, the message of the document is readily absorbed by the reader's mind, even if the reader is not particularly interested in the content" (McCain, 1992, p. 46).

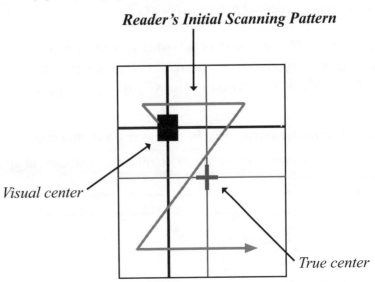

Reader's Initial Scanning Pattern

Visual center

True center

D-4 Redirecting a Reader's Attention

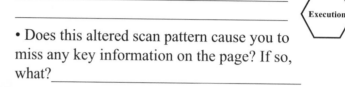

Directions: Look at the following magazine covers and answer the questions:

Boating On Long Island

JANUARY 2006

Where To Dock Your Boat On Long Island?
The Hottest Yacht Club On The Island.
Boating Around Long Island.

Figure A

1. In **Figure A**, which direction does the action photograph lead your eye?

_____

_____

• Does this altered scan pattern cause you to miss any key information on the page? If so, what?_____

_____

2. Why do you want to scan **Figure B** more than once? _____

_____

_____

• How does the publisher redirect your attention to the Visual Center? _____

_____

_____

• How does the publisher organize the page so the images and text work together to emphasize the feature article? _____

_____

_____

_____

See how powerful lines, images, and graphics can force your eye to abandon its natural scanning pattern?

Holistic Healers Future in Medicine

Alternative Medicine, Answer or Hoax?

Learning More About Reflexology

Herbal Teas & Headaches?

Figure B

Notice how the *Holistic Healers* publisher strategically placed the man looking up at the key feature of this issue's publication, "Alternative Medicine, Answer or Hoax?"

*Remember the *Surfing on Fire Island* cover on Handout D-2?

Now can you explain why the boy is holding the surfboard at an angle rather than vertically?

_____

_____

The "Hot Areas" of a Page

Using the visual center, you can divide a page into four quadrants. Each quadrant of a cover page serves a different purpose, depending on the amount of time the reader's eye spends there and its order in the eye's natural scanning pattern. In his book *Designing for Communication: The Key to Successful Desktop Publishing*, McCain defines the "hot areas" of the page where the eye lingers (1992).

The table below is based on many of the principles Ted McCain discusses in his book. It helps students identify the quadrants and provides tips on how to best use each quadrant in the layout of a cover page.

The Four Quadrants

Quadrant (Approximate location)	Time spent	How to best utilize the quadrant in a cover page
1	35 %	Key components of the layout, like the main idea. Headlines or captivating photographs are usually placed here.
2	25%	Support the main idea. Introduce secondary themes.
3	25%	Support the main idea. Introduce secondary themes.
4	15%	Although it receives the least amount of time, it deserves attention. It leaves a lasting impression with the reader. Use this space to keep the reader's focus on the page or redirect it back to the visual center.

Appropriate Visual Expression

Another fundamental principle of design is the use of visual expressions—to communicate the theme of the written words and to leave the reader with a lasting visual memory.

Photographs, color schemes, charts, illustrative diagrams, lines, and graphic artwork can dramatically enhance and complement written text when used correctly. But if used haphazardly, these visual expressions can distract the reader from the text's main idea. When visual expressions don't work, it is often because they are inconsistent with the tone of the rest of the publication.

Remember, visual expression is most effective when it is consistent with the tone and meaning of the text it accompanies—and when it is used in moderation. Make sure your students don't get carried away. But there is a lot of room for artistic freedom when using visual expression. In fact, many consider this aspect of the publisher's role the most creative. So you and your students should have some fun with it! Distribute Handout D-5 and talk about each of the elements that make up visual expression.

D-5 Types of Visual Expression

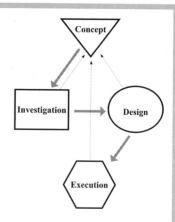

Visual expression in a publication consists of a lot of different elements.

The table below provides you with some guidelines for using visual expression effectively.

Guidelines for Using Visual Expressions

Visual Expression	Guideline
Images (photographs, original artwork)	Images should communicate a concept more powerfully than words. If you can, use photographs or your own artwork rather than clip art.
Color	• Warm colors (red, orange, yellow) grab the reader's attention. • Cool colors (blue, green, purple) produce a calming effect.
Balance	Graphics of equal size create a static, balanced page; objects of unequal size create a dynamic, lively publication. Either can be appropriate, depending on the style and tone of the publication.
Contrast	Contrast naturally stimulates the brain, which causes the reader to focus on the publication for a longer period of time. Publishers often contrast tones, shapes, and colors to achieve this effect.
Lines	Lines direct the flow of the publication and manipulate the order in which objects are viewed on the page. Lines can be either visible (printed) or invisible (not printed, but achieved by the deliberate placement of objects on the page).
Illustrative Diagrams	Illustrative diagrams are used to convey complex concepts or operations to the reader in a visual format. Illustrative diagrams clarify ideas and serve as visual references for the information.

A note about tone: The publication's tone is integral to its central idea; therefore, the publication's organization, visual expression, and written text must all communicate one consistent tone. They must all support the same main idea. Ted McCain gives a great example of developing tonal unity or stylistic unity:

"An advertisement for a new high tech car with aerodynamic styling would call for a design that was exciting and futuristic. Using an Old English typeface for a title would be out of place. The reader would be confused and communication would be compromised."

From *Designing for Communication: The Key to Successful Desktop Publishing*, by T. McCain, 1992, p. 55.

Below are two great magazine covers you can share with your students. Read the notes aloud and discuss how the covers demonstrate the importance of visual expression on a cover page.

Setting the Tone with Visual Expression

In this *Extreme Sports* cover, visual expression sets the tone. The publisher uses visual expression to grab your attention before you even have an opportunity to read the text, drawing your eyes to the visual objects on the page.

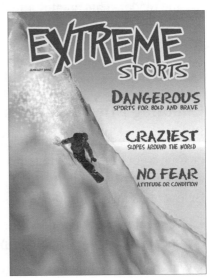

Think about these items as you examine the cover of *Extreme Sports*:

- This action photograph captures a moment in time of the snowboarder's extreme activity. The aggressive motion of the snowboarder creates an adventurous tone.

- The light appears to be coming from the top, casting a shadow downward. This gives the page a sense of speed and motion—and leads your eyes down the page.

- The bold fonts used for the headlines and featured articles also contribute to the adventurous tone.

- Notice the words that highlight the feature articles: *Dangerous*, *Craziest*, and *No Fear*. What kind of emotions do these words inspire?

The Effects of Contrasting Visual Expression

Contrast is one of the most powerful tools you can use to emphasize objects on a page. Publishers use various forms of contrast to stimulate their readers, to get them to react to their publications. This reaction helps readers form lasting memories of the subject matter.

Examine how the publisher of this *Skateboarding Weekly* magazine uses contrasts in aspects like size, shape, and lighting to give this cover a "wow" effect:

- **Size** – The publisher uses an unusual camera angle, shooting from ground level, to distort the size of the ramp and the rider.

- **Shape** – The shapes are also altered by the photography choices. Notice how the light pole on the right side seems to lean.

- **Light Concentration** – The natural light source originates from above, casting the darkest shadows in the bottom left of the photo. The shadows at the bottom of the page also contribute to the illusion of extreme altitude. The lighting moves your eye toward the top of the page, spotlighting the rider.

- **Lines** – Lines direct the flow of the publication. "All your life you have been trained to follow lines and not to cross them. This training, plus the eye's natural tendency to follow graphic lines, gives lines considerable power to direct the movement of the eye" (McCain, 1992, p. 50). Notice how the lines on the ramp direct your eye back toward the title of the magazine.

- **Contrast** – Contrast, like the black and white stripes of the ramp, is a great way to keep the reader interested in the publication. "Contrasting sizes can create visual tension, which helps keep the reader interested" (Parker, 1998, p. 13).

- **Balance** – The publisher also uses an informal balance or dynamic balance. "Larger, heaver objects must be placed nearer the center of the page and smaller, lighter objects must be placed further away from the center to maintain balance. Informal balance creates visual tension and arouses curiosity in the reader. This creates a feeling of excitement, surprise, energy, and life in designs" (McCain, 1992, p. 39). The publisher places the large ramp in the center of the page and a smaller ramp to the left side of the page. This creates informal or dynamic balance and excites the viewer.

Choosing Effective Colors

Your students should carefully plan what colors they will use. A good color scheme consists of three or four colors that work together, creating continuity and an aesthetically pleasing appearance. Some colors work better together than others, so it is important to have an understanding of color relationships. Below are some common color schemes that employ basic color relationships:

- **Grayscale** shades are good for black and white printing; designing in this color scheme provides your students with a predictable print output.

- **Warm** colors—like red, orange, and yellow—imply action and are good attention-getters.

- **Cool** colors—like blue, green, and purple—are effective for producing a more subtle effect (Burmark, 2002, p. 38).

- **Triad** color schemes are another effective use of color relationships; they utilize a balance of the three primary colors: red, yellow, and blue.

Remember, students should maintain consistent color schemes throughout their projects to create a professional end product. While students can be creative and deviate slightly from the color schemes mentioned here, it is imperative that they keep the number of colors down—to a maximum of three or four that complement each other and support the tone the students want to project.

Powerful Text Messages

In the previous section, you and your students learned how visual expression works within the organization and tone of the publication. Written words must also work within these guidelines. In this section, you and your students will examine not only how headings, subheadings, and captions fit within the organizational structure of publications, but also how they grab the readers' attention, arouse emotion, and deliver the essence of the publication with compelling words.

The two primary components of quality headings, subheadings, and captions included here are tone and font type.

Tone

Headlines, subheadings, and captions are the publisher's most effective way of setting the tone of a page. While images are capable of arousing emotion on their own, the words define the central theme of the page and sway the reader's point of view toward the publisher's subject matter.

Headings are one of the most powerful tools a publisher can use to convince the reader to read the entire publication.

When you and your students work with headings, and any text for that matter, one choice you're always faced with is what type of font to use.

Font Type

Contrary to popular belief, font type, size, and attributes (such as bold, italics, and underlines) are chosen for specific functions—*not* just because a publisher likes them. These physical characteristics provide publishers another way to control the order and pace in which people read their publications. Like the page characteristics you've learned about that can promote fluent scanning, there are font characteristics that influence a reader's ability to read fluently—specifically to recognize words.

The following sections review some effective practices for formatting text, explaining how to use fonts to lead readers through a publication.

Choosing the Best Font Type

To choose the style of font that works best for a certain task, remind your students of these three facts:

1. A reader's eyes scan across words horizontally, sweeping from left to right across the page.
2. A reader's ability to read quickly is based on immediate word recognition. Word recognition is improved when a word can be recognized by the reader skimming its top half.
3. The font style must be appropriate for its function. A *serif* font is appropriate for text bodies, and a *sans serif* font is appropriate for long-distance reading and headlines.

Distribute Handout D-6 to your students and discuss.

Review the difference between *serif* and *sans serif* fonts and the appropriate use of attributes like bold, italics, and underlines, including the following suggestions:

- "Bold is excellent for longer points because the basic shape of the characters is not altered. Thus the type is still readable" (McCain, 1992, p. 104).
- Don't use italics for more than 10–12 words (McCain, p. 104).
- "Underlining interferes with the reader's ability to recognize letter forms" (Parker, 1998, p. 54).

Note: The table on Handout D-6 can act as a quick reference guide for your students when they are putting together their publications or presentations.

D-6 Choosing Font Types and Attributes

There are many different types of fonts, but for general purposes, they can all be divided into two families: *serif* and *sans serif*.

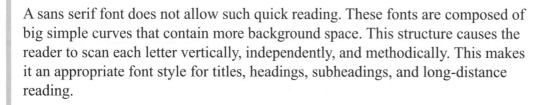

sans serif

A *serif* is a slight projection at the extremities of a printed letter. A serif font makes reading the body of a text easier because the serifs on the letters create the horizontal line that our eye searches for when trying to read quickly and continuously.

A sans serif font does not allow such quick reading. These fonts are composed of big simple curves that contain more background space. This structure causes the reader to scan each letter vertically, independently, and methodically. This makes it an appropriate font style for titles, headings, subheadings, and long-distance reading.

• Which font type do you think is better for a newspaper column?

• Which font type do you think is better for an EXIT sign?

_____

The table below lists some other stylistic attributes you may want to keep in mind when using text.

Font Attributes

Attribute	Effect	Do Use...	Do Not Use...
Bold	Slows the reader down by pulling the eye **toward** the **bold type**	In **headings** and subheadings	For emphasis within a sentence or body of a text.
Italics	Simulates *spoken* words	For *emphasis* within a sentence or *body of a text* For kickers, *captions,* long quotations	In titles and headings
Underline	<u>Slows the reader down</u>	For emphasis, in titles and captions	For emphasis within a sentence or body of a text.

What's the Big Idea?

Before your students start getting too involved with the details for their projects, you may want to remind them to spend a few minutes thinking about the main objective of their knowledge entities.

You may want to have these questions written on the board as a "do now" and have students answer them in their journals:

• What is the point of this project?
• What should listeners know or be able to do as a result of experiencing the project?

Also have your students consider what form, what type of purpose, the project will have:

• Will it be informative?
• Will it be persuasive?
• Or will it be interactive?

Once your students have answered these questions, they will have a better idea about where their projects are headed. Have them use CmapTools or another graphic organizer to start outlining the ideas they want to include about the concept.

Assessing Student Progress

Your students have learned a lot about design principles. This is a good time to review what they've learned. On the next page is a checklist for you to use when assessing your students' design work.

You may want to provide this checklist to your students before they continue with their projects, so they clearly understand how you will be evaluating their designs. For that reason, the checklist is provided as a separate page that you can easily copy and distribute.

Global Design Principles Checklist

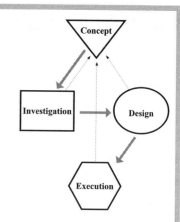

Directions: Use the following checklist to help guide and assess your students' designs. Check off each item that the student performs proficiently.

Makes notes of any questions you have as you review the student's work.

_____ Does the student use the visual center of the page wisely?

_____ Does the student utilize the quadrants in the cover page wisely? Does the student strike a nice balance?

_____ Does the student use contrast and lines effectively? How are they used?

_____ What illustrative diagrams does the student use to convey complex concepts or operations to the reader in a visual format?

_____ Does the student use effective colors to help portray the message?

_____ Does the student use a powerful text message?

_____ Does the student use an appropriate font for the tone and mood of the project?

_____ Does the design of the project fit the student's original intent? (For example, if the student wanted to be informative, is the design well suited for that task?)

6. Blueprint Time

Now that your students have had adequate time to grapple with and investigate the concept, it is imperative that they synthesize all of their ideas and begin to start envisioning the final form of their project. In other words, they need to plan.

Gathering information helped them to learn about their topic. Planning is the next step in learning how to execute a successful knowledge entity. During the planning phase, they decide on the details that will help them get ready to create a knowledge entity that represents their understanding of the topic.

During the planning, or blueprint, phase, skillful visual architects do the following:

- Review their prewriting visual diagram.
- Review the details they have collected during the Investigation phase.
- Select one of the project choices described in the Design section.
- Summarize the Global Design Principles.
- Think of an interesting focus.
- Organize their details in the most effective way to support or develop their project focus.

Sketching Initial Ideas

Before having your students turn on their computer and begin creating their own projects using the step-by-step instructions included in the Execution section of this handbook, give your students some time to sketch their initial ideas by hand.

They should develop more than one page layout for their design, using the Global Design Principles as guidelines. They should experiment with different items to put in the visual center of the page and the different types of fonts they could use to ensure readability and consistency.

You May Ask ... Why Not Plan on the Computer?

Sketching by hand is a lot quicker than planning on the computer. Repositioning or changing images goes a lot quicker in sketches. In addition, drawing also lets students easily compare and contrast the different styles and designs they have created.

The following pages include guides to help your students prepare their research papers, presentations, publications, movies, and photo slide shows. You can copy and distribute these pages to your students as guidelines, but your students should feel free to create their own as well.

Coming Up Next:
- Outlining Presentations and Papers
- Designing Publications
- Creating Production Storyboards
- Planning Photo Albums and Essays

Design

D-7 Outlines: Organizing Your Presentation

Directions: Review the following when you're ready to start organizing your presentation.

Informative Presentation Outline

I.   Introduction: Briefly outline your complete understanding of the topic in an interesting fashion

    A.   Use illustrations, charts, video clips, or other graphic art that will help give your audience an understanding of the big picture.

    B.   Include general comments or facts that will hook your audience.

    C.   Introduce your thesis statement.

II. Body: Provide three or four specific points that support your thesis.

    A.   Present each point on its own slide, with a few powerful words and pictures.

    B.   Include details about the points.

III. Conclusion: Restate or reword your thesis.

    A.   Summarize your key points.

    B.   Leave your audience with a picture or a startling statement to consider after you're done.

Persuasive Presentation Outline

I.   Introduction: Provide a brief overview of your topic and why it is controversial.

    A.   Explain both sides of the argument.

    B.   Introduce your thesis statement.

    Note: Choose one side of the fence and stay on it. Many people can see both sides of an issue; however, to persuade your audience, you must choose one side and develop a logical argument to support it.

II. Body: Provide three or four specific arguments that support your thesis. Each slide should contain a persuasive argument that supports your thesis statement.

    A.   Statistics – You may want to find some statistics about your topic and add a chart, graph, or other visual form to represent the statistics in your presentation.

    B.   Expert Testimony – Quotes from experts in the field is another great tactic to use when developing and designing a persuasive presentation.

    C.   Comparision – If you can make a comparision to the way people do things in one time period or culture as compared to the way they are doing things here and now, it gives people an opportunity to relate to the information.

III. Conclusion: Restate or reword your thesis.

    A.   Restate the main arguments in your persuasive speech.

    B.   Think of an original way to get people on your side of the argument. This is your last chance, so make sure you put some thought into your last slide.

D-7 Outlines: Organizing Your Presentation (cont.)

Interactive Presentation Outline

I.   Introduction: Create a "do now" activity for your classmates to get them interacting with each other and thinking about the subject matter.

    A.   With your first slide, start an activity or ask questions that engage your audience with your topic.

    B.   Provide the audience a few minutes to work on the questions or activity. Then ask the audience members for their feedback.

    C.   Record their input in the Meeting Minutes option that is available to you in PowerPoint.

    D.   Introduce your thesis by making comparisions with the input you just received.

II. Body: Provide three or four specific points that support your thesis.

    A.   Prepare a slide to explain each point.

    B.   Add visual aids like graphs, illustrations, and charts to illustrate your points.

III. Wrap-Up

    A.   Develop questions or activities that engage the audience again—to think about the new material that was presented during the presentation.

    B.   Record the audience members' responses.

    C.   Compare these responses with the responses provided at the beginning of class.

    D.   As a group, reflect if anything new was uncovered and whether any audience members changed their opinions from the beginning of the presentation.

Outlining Presentations and Papers

An outline helps students organize their notes into an effective presentation or research paper. You may have to discuss with your students what an outline is. "An outline is an organized list of information you will use for the main part of your essay or report. In an outline, list details from general to specific" (Sebranek et al., 1999, p. 119).

You should review with your students how to label their main ideas with Roman numerals (e.g., I, II, III). Then, under each Roman numeral are supporting details labeled A, B, C, and so on. Discuss the guidelines on Handout D-7 for the various types of presentation outlines: informative, persuasive, and interactive. The same basic principles can be applied to more traditional research papers.

Designing Publications

Structure

All types of written publications, including novels, newspapers, magazine articles, instruction manuals, lab reports, poetry, magazine covers, and advertisements, are held together by their structure. Some types of publications, including newsletters and magazine covers, are bound by standard practices and conventions; others, such as advertisements and poetry, are open to a more freestyle structure.

In this section, we examine the conventions of newsletters and cover pages, and learn how their structure organizes the content and gives the reader a manageable breakdown of the material. Because of these structures, the reader is able to easily scan the entire document and preview the essential components before scouring the whole text. The structure also breaks down a whole topic into more specific and manageable subtopics, providing concise points for the reader, making the material easier to comprehend and retain.

In the following sections, we will examine the structure of newsletters and cover pages and learn effective techniques to make the structure both pleasing to the eye and helpful for the reader.

After reviewing with your students the different structures that newsletters and cover pages may take, you may want to give your students about 20 minutes to begin sketching on a blank sheet of paper a blueprint for their publication. You should circulate around the room asking students questions about their plans while they work. Depending on your style and the learning needs of your students, they can work individually at their desks to create their blueprints, in pairs, or in groups of four. Students can finish their blueprints as a homework assignment.

Newsletters

Newsletters are a common publication that promotes activities, happenings, and other public relations information for a particular organization or interest group. Newsletters are usually published in regular intervals (e.g., monthly, quarterly), and they appeal to a specific target group or membership. They typically contain articles, editorials, images, a mission statement about the publishing organization, and contact information for the publishers—all set within a stylized format that includes the organization's logo or slogan.

D-8 Dissecting a Newsletter

The Front Page

The front page of a newsletter is the first impression the reader gets of the entire publication, so it is critical that the cover page entices the reader to browse the newsletter. From a structural standpoint, the cover page contains a captivating lead article and a glimpse of other featured articles or components of the newsletter. It also reflects the tone of the organization and often gives insight into the organization's purpose.

Remember the principles of design you learned about? You want to consider these principles when creating the cover page of your newsletter. Carefully select your font type and pictures, and ensure all these elements work together to set the tone for your newsletter.

Review the *Providence Digest* example on the next page to learn about the standard parts of the front page.

Inside Pages

The inside pages of a newsletter usually contain two to six articles written in column format, which are usually accompanied by images, graphs, pull quotes, and other visual devices supporting the articles. Keep in mind that adjoining pages (e.g., pages 2 and 3) should be treated as one because the reader will see them both at once. Use the same style of layout on both pages and make sure they are balanced.

Create a thumbnail sketch of the inside of your newsletter. Decide which article should be placed where and who should author each article. Keep the tone, color schemes, and font type the same as the cover page. Remember your tone should be consistent throughout the newsletter.

The Back Cover

The back cover of a newsletter usually contains information about the publishing organization:
• A mission statement
• The business address and contact information
• A list of staff members or contributors to the newsletter
• Space for a mailing label if it is to be mailed to its readers
• An article or feature that is light and witty

Newsletters that are designed as a school assignment might include these items, in addition to or replacing the "publishing organization" information:
• The objective of the assignment
• The teacher name, course name, and period number
• A list of group members and their roles

Remember to lay out the back cover in your thumbnail sketches. Doing this will help ensure that your group reviewed the assignment's objective carefully and that each group member's roles and responsibilities are clearly defined.

D-8 Dissecting a Newsletter (cont.)

College Weekly

Vol. 1. Issue 1. January 1, 2006

Nameplate: *This contains the title, volume, issue, and date of the publication. Notice how the title font is consistent with the tone of the organization.*

Classified

Realestate

Travel

Jobs

Post Print Ads

Education

News

Top Stories

World news

Sports

Campus News

Helath/Science

Entertainment

Weather

Columnists

Editorials

Excellence In Education
written by John Doe

Lead article: This is the most significant article in the newsletter and gets the most prominent position on the cover page. The title usually appears near the page's visual center.

What happens when two premier institutes of excellence come together... and facility ex... ...ping to happen ...gether.

A ...x and USC S... ...ity's College. As... ...nitially focus or... ...rs in infor-m... ...logy and, especially, engineering management.

The University's College's Distance Education Network, one of the foremost distance education facilities in engineering education, will play a key role in this tie-up. According to CL dean of College," The VSE is the academic home of 23 members of National Academy of Engineering, one of the two engineering schools in the US that is home to two National Science Foundation-funded Engineering Research Centre: the Intergrated Media Systems Centre

Table of contents: The TOC lays out the organization of the newsletter and helps the reader find regular features and interesting articles.

...hich is the birth place ...lame System and ...10 engineering prog-...mong private uni-...three engineering ...in the emerging fields of solid-state electronics, communication, signal processing, controls and computer engineering is well known across the world" An initiative of the VP and founder of infoUSA and a distinguished alumnus and life time fellow of other school management, the tie up will take place in different areas particularly at Post Graduate (PG) level. The dean said" We have outlined four key areas of collaberation, which include joint research, distance-learning programms, and student faculty exchange at PG leve. The school is not going to be the only beneficiary of the tie-up, as the 19 departments, eight Centres of Excellence and three schools too are going to beneift from it." Senior Vice President, while commenting on the tie-up said, ...ts. ...ross ...ed-...r's... ...g. 10)

"In This Issue" or other attention-getter: This section highlights points of interest contained within the newsletter. It should make the reader want to continue browsing the newsletter.

BASKETBALL

STUDENT Vs. UCS

pg. 11

STUDENT ACTIVITIES

Theater class annouces new play!!!

pg. 8

DECEMBER						
				1	2	3
4	5	6	7	8	9	10
11	12	13	14	15	16	17
18	19	20	21	22	23	24
25	26	27	28	29	30	31

JANUARY						
1	2	3	4	5	6	7
8	9	10	11	12	13	14
15	16	17	18	19	20	21
22	23	24	25	26	27	28
29	30	31				

Alumni Donations
written by Jane Doe

Secondary article: This is the second-most significant article and therefore gets the second-most prominent position on the cover page.

...cern of any institution. The University's University's current alumni giving rate is 29 percent, which ranks it 27th among universities in the most recent U.S. News and World Report college rankings. Princeton University leads with a 60 percent giving rate."Alumni giving is an institutional priority, often called 'job one' by the President and trustees," said Mia Mills, associate director of annual giving at Princeton University, about their succes in alumni donation efforts.

The U of C's relatively low rate among peer academic institutions has raised concern particular in recent year, with the number of donors ... ..

(continued pg.5)

A good newsletter is informative to the reader and also fun to read and browse through. It is important that the articles are complemented by lighter material such as fun facts, word games, and graphics that offer a variety of activities to connect with the different personal interests of their target audience.

Distribute Handout D-8 to your students and discuss the major components of a newsletter. They can use this handout as a guide when they create thumbnail sketches of each of the sections for their own newsletters.

In their groups, students should discuss the following questions as they outline their newsletter:
- Who is in charge of writing which article?
- Which article should appear first? Which article should appear second? Why is this the correct order?
- Is there a better way to lay out this newsletter?
- What fun facts should be added to the newsletter?
- And finally, do we have enough engaging pictures to make this newsletter appealing?

The Cover Page

Although the magazine cover page appears to be one of the simplest project choices available, it is actually rather complicated. You have only one page to set a tone, engage the reader, identify the main attraction or lead article, and use power words and teasers to engage readers, as well as introduce the magazine title and publishing organization.

Distribute Handout D-9 to your students and discuss the steps to creating a successful and attractive cover page.

Students should also take this opportunity to lay out the background of their covers. Often overlooked, backgrounds are an integral part of a dynamic cover page. Underneath the foreground objects, backgrounds, which can be composed of photographs, images, text, clip art, logos, or color patterns, can
- add continuity to the page,
- contribute greatly to the tone of the page, and
- help grab the reader's attention.

Before letting your students get started on creating their own cover pages, you may want to carefully check their thumbnail sketches to ensure their covers match your objective. It is crucial that students really take the time to think through their work. They have only one page with a limited amount of text to demonstrate their thorough understanding of a topic.

Some students may select the cover page format because it appears to be the least amount of work. They don't understand how much foresight goes into planning a magazine cover page, and they may have a hard time demonstrating mastery of the material using only key terms and phrases. The more time you spend with them on their thumbnail sketches, the better students tend to do on the final project.

You may also want to add a writing component to this piece, to assess their understanding and new knowledge about the concept.

D-9 Creating a Magazine Cover Page

Directions: Follow these steps to create a successful and attractive cover page.

1. Find the visual center of the page. You may want to make a note of it lightly with a pencil.

2. Review your notes about natural page-scanning patterns. You may find it helpful to draw a light pencil mark of a "Z" on your cover page.

3. Identify the "hot areas" of the page. You may want to mark these areas with asterisks.

4. Decide on an appropriate tone and font(s) for your cover page. Review your notes about visual expression and font types. Note here why you made your specific choices.

_____

_____

5. Find a dynamic and appropriate graphic, picture, or illustration to catch your reader's attention. Describe the graphic here and explain why you feel it is an effetive choice for your cover.

_____

_____

6. Choose power words carefully, to entice potential readers and convey your material.

_____

_____

_____

_____

Don't forget about the background!

Backgrounds can accomplish many tasks, like these:

• Illustrate your main attraction or lead article.

• Enhance the tone of your publication—by adding color, light, shading, or contrast.

• Supply a lively and contrasting backdrop for the items in the cover's foreground.

You can create a background with photographs, images, text, clip art, logos, or color patterns.

Creating Production Storyboards

In her book *Visual Literacy: Learn to See, See to Learn,* Lynell Burmark talks about learning while creating movies:

> One of my favorite software programs from the Edmark-Riverdeep Corporation, Millie & Bailey Kindergarten, has an activity where students "Make a Movie." They rearrange a sequence of three or four frames and then tell the projectionist to roll the film: Lights, camera, action! Cinematographers refer to this movie-making process as "storyboarding." The flow of the action and the story lines are mapped out as a sequence of thumbnail images representing scenes in the show. Programs like PowerPoint make it easy to reorder thumbnails in the slide view mode. (Burmark, 2002, p. 88)

This is a great way of introducing storyboarding to students in elementary school, but a similar exercise can also be done with older students. Burmark explains how Jerome Burg does a version of this activity with his high-school class. He divides the class up into teams; each team chooses a novel and has to reduce that novel to four cartoon panels. "They discuss issues of plot, character development, and critical action and argue about which elements must be drawn for someone who has not read the book to be able to follow the story" (Burmark, 2002, p. 89). Students then select the words that must be included in the voice balloons that reveal the character's emotions, motives, and personality.

This is a great way to introduce storyboarding to your students. If your students have just read a novel or learned about a historical event or new math concept, you could ask them to communicate their knowledge in three or four pictures, explaining the story, event, or concept to another person. You could also use this as a preparatory activity for students storyboarding their knowledge entities.

Storyboard Overview

Storyboards need to be created for whatever type of movie production you and your students decide to produce. Explain to students that storyboards help a producer create a sequential road map for their production and visualize its sequence and delivery. Storyboards also serve as a communication tool for the members in the production team. The storyboard acts like a set of directions explaining to the team where they should stand, where the shot will be taken, what time of day the footage will be shot, who is in each scene, what they should be doing in each scene, and what type of costumes they should be wearing. In addition, the storyboard helps the director know when the scene is over and what type of emotion is supposed to be portrayed, and instructs the videoographer how to put together the movie, including what transitions, fonts, and music to use. In short, storyboards are complex and require a lot of time to be done well.

Handwritten vs. PowerPoint

Many storyboards are handwritten. Students simply divide a blank sheet of paper into six boxes, for example: three boxes on the top and three boxes on the bottom. They then use pencil to sketch their storyboards in the boxes.

Tech-savvy students can create their storyboards in PowerPoint. They open a blank slide in PowerPoint and use the Draw toolbar to sketch their actors' and actresses' positions and movements and to envision the setting. One advantage to using PowerPoint to create the storyboards is that the entire crew can view the storyboard. It becomes a working document, and slides can be easily shifted in the transition mode. It is also easy to print out multiple copies for the crew members. Students can even e-mail the storyboard to each other, so they each have an opportunity to work on it.

Typical Storyboard Contents

Each box, or slide, in a storyboard should contain the following information:

- **Physical Environment** – The set design/location

- **Spatial Quality** – Staging, camera angle, camera lens, the movement of any elements in the shot

- **Transition Types** – Transitions used between each slide in your iMovie

- **Sound Effects** – Dialogue, background music (Music should be chosen carefully, as it determines the rhythm and tone of the movie.)

- **List of Crew Members** – Which actors and actresses are needed to complete each scene

For more tips on creating storyboards, visit Apple's education page: http://education.apple.com/ education/ilife/howto. On the right-hand side of the Web page, under "Making Great Movies," click on the link for "helpful tips and techniques." You will find great tips for storyboarding your movies here. (You can also access the site directly at http://education.apple.com/education/ilife/howto/iMovie_tips/ index.php.)

This would make a great homework assignment for your students. Two days before you begin storyboarding in class, have your students access the Apple tips on making a movie. Students should visit the Web page and take notes. Then students can use the instructions provided here, along with their own notes, to make a cool new production.

The First Slide

The first slide created by your students is extremely important. It introduces and sets the tone of the entire production, with visuals and sounds. For example, if your student is creating a horror movie, he should find some eerie music and a scary image. He could even select a spooky type of font to further enhance the overall tone of the production. Your students must be careful that all of their choices on the first slide of their storyboard contribute to one overall tone, which will then be carried throughout the entire production.

Students can work in pairs or groups when they start creating their storyboards. You should guide them through the first couple of slides of the storyboard. The first slide should contain the following components: title (and font type), visual, and music selection. Students should draw a box and sketch the location of their visuals. The title of the production and the type of music that is playing should be written in the lower right-hand corner.

Transitions in the Storyboard

You may want to discuss with your students the different types of transitions that are available to them when they are creating their storyboards. Make a list of transition types on the board. Discuss what transitions may be best suited to represent different events occurring throughout the movie. Have students decide what types of transitions could work for events such as these:

- A change in location
- A lapse in time
- An introduction to a new character

For example, some students may feel that a push transition works best for the scenery changes; other students may feel that a ripple effect would work better. Let students decide for themselves what type of transitions to use, but remind them that they must consistently use the same transition throughout the entire production for that event.

Student should select a maximum of three types of transitions for their movie. The transitions should be consistently used, representing the same film movements or shifts, throughout the entire production. Have students write their transitions between each slide in their storyboard.

The Sound of Music

"Sound is the most frequently overlooked ingredient in presentations. But the quality of the audio track can either make or break the show … music inserted at just the right moment can evoke any emotion; exciting sounds can enhance a story of visual presentation" (Simkins et al., 2002, p. 19). You may want your students to consider the following questions about the type of music that should be included in their production. Write the questions on the board and have the students discuss them in groups or journal about them:

- When is it appropriate to include music in a scene? When should the music be heard only as background filler?
- How do you decide what type of music should be playing?
- When should the music contain singing? When should the music be purely instrumental?
- When should the music overpower the words spoken by the actors and actresses?

Blueprinting Fictional Storyboards

In fictional storyboards, the first slide is not the title slide, but rather a slide containing a list of characters and a brief description describing their roles and personalities. The next slide provides a brief sketch of the tone, font size and type, and transition types to be used in the production. Then comes the title slide. A creative way to begin a video story is to start with an outside shot of the first location. Have the producer plan the exposition of the fictional storyboard and get ready to introduce the characters. Then show the list of characters and continue from there.

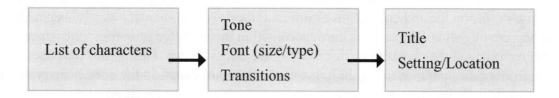

The Exposition

Every fictional story contains exposition. The exposition of the story focuses on allowing the audience to become more intimate with the characters and to learn about their personalities, through action and dialogue. Just as important, the exposition also includes the beginning of the plot. Remind your students that, as producers, they should start giving their audience subtle hints on how the plot, or story line, unfolds; however, they don't want to give away the ending.

Sample Exposition Storyboard Boxes

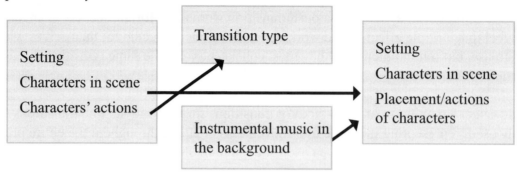

Complications and the Resolution

The next set of slides included in the storyboard should focus on the characters trying to find a resolution to their conflict. The highest point of interest in the fictional video story is known as the *climax*. It is when the conflict reaches its peak. Music, when included appropriately here, can create a highly dramatic effect. The story is concluded when the loose ends are tied up: the *resolution*. Music can be used very effectively here as well, to make a point or to create drama.

Slides in this part of the storyboard will look a lot like the slides in the exposition segment. Each slide should have a description of the setting, a list of characters, their actions, the music included, and finally how one slide transitions to the next. See the sample below.

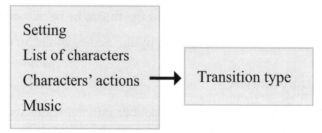

The last slide of the storyboard contains rolling credits. Remind your students to be careful about choosing the music that plays during the credits, as it leaves a lasting impression on the audience.

Blueprinting Documentary Storyboards

A documentary is a nonfiction movie that is written to share the events of someone's life, describe a historical event, or inform the audience about a particular topic. A documentary usually begins by a narrator reading the title slide. The topic is introduced within the next five minutes as the narrator presents a brief overview of the events to be discussed in the documentary. During this introduction, still images flash in front of the audience to highlight the most important events in the documentary. Many documentaries also include instrumental background music during this introduction.

Timing the still images that appear as the narrator introduces the subject matter can be tricky. Each image must appear right before the narrator is ready to talk about it. The narrator should pause to allow the audience a few seconds to connect to the next image.

It appears that an audience will remember more of a presentation if they are given the chance to look at each new slide for a few seconds before the speaker begins speaking. People need to bring their own emotions and life experiences to the image before they are ready to hear what the image means to you. Let the image sink in first; then you can hang your message onto the visual hook. (Burmark, 2002, p. 68)

In many documentaries, the narrator's first words are something like "Join us in the next hour …" as the background music begins to fade and a slide show of still images starts. Events are usually introduced in sequential matter. Different experts are asked to give their opinion on the subject matter here as well. As each expert speaks, his or her name and title is written on the screen below his or her picture.

Remind your students that they should plan on getting experts involved in their documentaries. They need to make arrangements to videotape them, as well as prepare questions for their interviews. (If students can't arrange for a live interview with an expert, they can choose to show a still image of the expert and do a voice-over mimicking the expert's voice.)

Another technique used by documentary producers is to film two experts in the same room together, debating the topic. If your students have an opportunity to film a debate, make sure the camera person positions the camera to record about two-thirds of the podium and the heads of the debaters. The producer may want to encourage the debaters to use their hands while they talk, to engage the audience more. The camera person may also want to include a few shots of the audience while the debate is taking place: This helps to share the intimacy of the debate setting with the documentary viewers. Remind students that while they are shooting a debate, the background setting needs to be quiet and a microphone is sometimes needed to capture the debaters' voices on tape. (Students who can't arrange for a live debate between experts can reenact a debate. This is actually a great way for them to learn both sides of an argument and to practice their persuasive speaking skills.)

Sample Documentary Storyboard

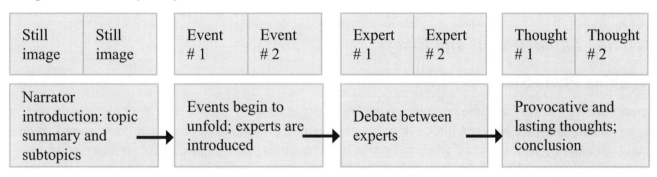

Blueprinting Commercial Storyboards

Commercials are primarily produced to convince the viewer to believe in a product. Commercial producers carefully select an advertising appeal that best engages their target audience. They hope to stamp a memory in their viewers' minds. Commercials usually last about 30 seconds, so the producer needs to carefully plan each video shot to display a lot of emotion and make a lasting impression.

First, the commercial producer must decide on a target audience and decide how to engage this audience as soon as the commercial opens. With 30 seconds to sell a product, the producer needs the audience to be engaged and paying attention from the very beginning. For example, if the commercial was advertising a toothpaste for kids, one of the first shots in the commercial would probably be a shot of a happy kid brushing his teeth with that product.

Commercial producers try to appeal to their audiences using many different techniques. These are three of the most popular: the humor appeal, the scientific appeal, and the bandwagon appeal.

In the *humor appeal*, each shot of the commercial is filled with lots of emotion. It uses music and transitions to keep the mood of the commercial fun and light.

With the *scientific appeal*, the producer will usually use a graph or a chart to demonstrate how the product is more successful than the competing brand. The scientific appeal also usually shows a visual of the product in action. The toothpaste commercial might show the tarter being lifted off the kid's teeth. And then it would show another brand of toothpaste leaving lots of tarter and decay on the teeth and in between the gums. The scientific appeal usually gives a quick technical explanation of why the product being advertised is more successful than the other brand.

Sample Commercial Storyboard (Scientific Appeal)

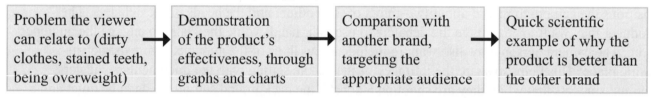

The *bandwagon appeal* is another successful appeal that many commercial producers employ. The idea behind the bandwagon appeal is that everybody is doing it; if you do it too, you will be happy like the rest of the group. To successfully employ this technique, the producer shows a group of people having a lot of fun using the product.

Planning Photo Albums and Essays

Designing Photo Shots

Pictures are a great way to share an experience, a moment in time, or a place with your classmates and other viewers. They are a great addition into any publication, presentation, or movie. Photographs spice up and personalize your students' work and projects. Sometimes photographers take so many good pictures that they use them to create a slide show.

The first step to helping your students create a great slide show is learning how to be a good photographer. A photographer uses images in these three major ways:
- to capture and share a moment in time with others
- to make a statement, and
- to capture a unique viewpoint of an object.

The following pages are filled with photography techniques that you can share with your students. Distribute and review Handout D-10, Learning to Become a Photographer. These student-friendly pages will have your students taking great pictures and using them to leave lasting impressions on their viewers in no time. Students should also have multiple copies of Handout D-11, A Photographer's Journal. They should complete one of these worksheets each time they take a picture. The journal pages should be gathered in a folder or bound, to be reviewed in the future.

Planning Slide Shows

Slide shows are a great way to share pictures with others. Your students should choose the best pictures they have that can tell a story on their own. Remember slide shows are usually introduced briefly; then the presenter turns on the slide show and let's the audience watch the show, without any further comment. After the slide show, there is usually a discussion period.

When your students have their photographs and are ready to blueprint their slide shows, instruct them to take all of the pictures and spread them out across the table or on the floor. They should first decide on the best order to present the pictures. Should they be in chronological order? Or does some other order, like cause and effect, make more sense?

After the students have put the images in order, they need to decide what kind of music should play during the show. Should it be a melancholy song, or should it be something upbeat? Have students brainstorm a number of options.

After the students have put together the slide show, as described in the Execution section, they will need to write an introductory speech. This speech should introduce the pictures and images that are going to be displayed in the slide show. They should also write the questions that they will ask at the conclusion of the slide show, to facilitate the audience discussion.

Assessing Student Progress

Your students are finally at the end of the Design phase of their projects. It is now time to formally evaluate their performance. On page 119 is a checklist for you to use when assessing your students' progress in this phase.

Remember, it can be helpful for students to have this information at the beginning of the lesson so they know what is expected of them. For that reason, the checklist is provided as a separate page that you can easily copy and distribute.

D-10 Learning to Become a Photographer

The three basic type of photographs that you will learn how to take are landscapes, action shots, and portraits (people shots). You will use different principles for each type, to make the photo more powerful. After you have mastered the principles discussed here, you may want to experiment with more artistic subjects, angles, and focal points.

Photography 101

Each photograph you take requires a different technique, style, and angle. So you are going to need to experiment with a variety of techniques and styles before choosing the picture that works best for you. Photographers keep a journal of the different techniques, shutter speeds, and times of day that they use (see Handout D-11). Recording this information helps them develop a repertoire of techniques that they can draw from when they are shooting new subjects.

Landscapes

The landscape photographer works mostly with light, distance, and camera positioning. The most dramatic landscape shots are taken when the sun is rising or setting. Landscape photographers usually wait until the sun is about 30 degrees above the horizon, as this angle makes for dramatic shadows and interesting pictures.

- When it is the right time of day to take your photograph, take a lot of shots of it. You may even want to take a shot of your landscape at different times of the day to see which pictures you like best.

- Use different types of lenses. Some lenses provide more depth between the landscape and the camera, while other lenses take close-up pictures.

- Experiment by moving your camera; take the picture from different angles. Focus on different items in the foreground. For example, if you are shooting a picture of the Eiffel Tower, a more interesting picture might be taken from either the left or right side of the tower, rather than from directly in front of it.

Action Shots

There are four major ways to take action shots: by freezing them, blurring them, panning them, or capturing them at the peak of their action.

Note: Many digital cameras have a manual-exposure mode so that you can alter the shutter speed. Please read the directions for your digital camera to learn how to use the manual-exposure mode.

- To freeze the action shot, take the picture at a fast shutter speed.

- To blur the action shot, use a slow shutter speed. Finding the right speed to blur the action just enough can be tricky. You'll need to practice and get used to the shutter speeds on your camera to feel comfortable achieving the balance needed for effective blurring.

D-10 Learning to Become a Photographer (cont.)

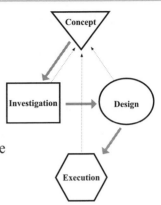

- To pan the action shot and create an artistic appearance, start tracking the subject as it is moving—before the moment you want to record. When the subject reaches the point when you want to begin recording, release the shutter and move the camera with the subject.

- To capture an action shot at the peak of the action, aim your camera where you expect the highest point of the action to be. Shoot when the subject hits that spot.

Shots of People

When your subject matter is a person, you want to make sure the person looks natural in the photograph. Posed pictures are trite and uninteresting, while candid shots capture raw emotion, making for much more interesting photographs.

Group shots can be even more interesting, as people are interacting with each other in a natural environment.

- The rule of thumb for taking pictures of people is to stand about four feet away. If you stand closer to your subject, the subject becomes elongated. Photographs taken farther away than four feet often make the subject appear flat.

- Another point to remember when taking pictures of people is to watch where the sun is—because the sun can affect the faces in your photograph. If the photograph is taken at noon, people in the picture are usually squinting, and their wrinkles are highlighted because of the sun's position directly overhead. It is ideal to capture the sun at 30 degrees, when it casts a soft light on the subject, and the light usually glimmers off their eyes.

- Take picture of your subjects at eye level. If your subject is shorter than you, crouch down to take the picture so you are at eye level. If you take a picture looking down, your subject is diminished in the picture.

Tracking Your Pictures

Record the technical information about your photographs using a copy of Handout D-11. Complete one of these sheets for each picture you take. Keep your journal pages together, so you can review them later.

This will help you keep track of the different shots and techniques that you have experimented with. Compare the different strategies you have used and reflect on which techniques were successful for you and which techniques you need to work on more.

Catalog your pictures into photo albums, with keywords and titles, so they are easy to locate later.

D-11 A Photographer's Journal

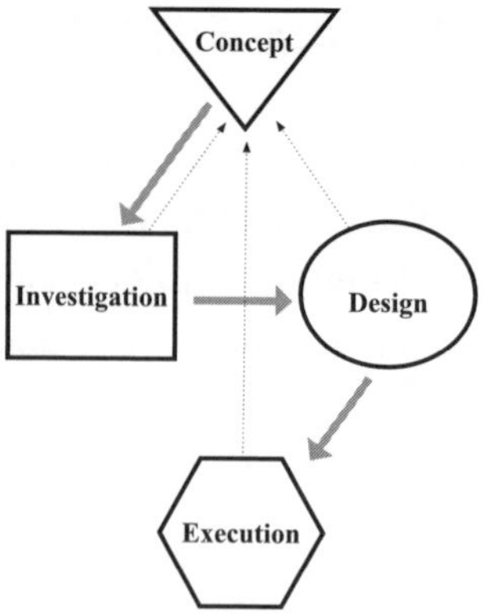

Directions: Use this sheet to record each picture you take.

1. Subject matter (e.g., identify the person, place, situation)

_____

_____

_____

_____

2. Time of day: _____

3. Angle from which I took the photograph: _____

4. Shutter speed:_____

5. Flash: On   Off   Automatic *(circle one)*

6. Other camera settings:

_____

_____

_____

_____

Additional Information for Action Shots

7. How much did the shutter speed blur or freeze the action shot?

_____

_____

_____

8. How fast was the subject moving?

_____

_____

_____

9. How did the subject's speed affect my shutter speed?

_____

_____

_____

_____

Project Blueprint Checklist

Directions: Use the following checklist to assess your students' blueprints. For each student's unique knowledge entity, select the appropriate statements below and evaluate the design accordingly.

_____ Ideas for the knowledge entity were sketched out.

_____ The presentation or paper is outlined according to Handout D-7.

_____ Newsletters are dissected into the front page, the inside pages, and the back cover page.

_____ Magazine covers follow the global design principles discussed.

_____ Storyboards contain the following information: physical environment, spatial quality, transition types, sound effects, and a list of crew members.

_____ Photo albums, photo essays, and slide shows use pictures that capture and share a moment in time with others, make a statement, and capture a unique viewpoint.

_____ The best pictures are chosen for photo albums, photo essays, and slide shows.

Works Cited

Burmark, L. (2002). *Visual literacy: Learn to see, see to learn.* Alexandria, VA: Association for Supervision and Curriculum Development.

McCain, T. (1992). *Designing for communication*: *The key to successful desktop publishing.* Eugene, OR: International Society for Technology in Education.

Parker, R. (1998). *Looking good in print* (4th ed.). Scottsdale, AR: Coriolis Group.

Sebranek, P., Kemper, D., & Meyer, V. (1999). *Write source 2000: A guide to writing, thinking, and learning.* Wilmington, MA: Great Source Education Group.

Simkins, M., Cole, K., Tavalin, F., & Means, B. (2002). *Increasing student learning through multimedia projects.* Alexandria, VA: Association for Supervision and Curriculum Development.

Execution

The Smooth Operator

Now that your students know what type of project they are going to do, they (and you) could probably use a few technical pointers.

A tech-savvy person can make multimedia products quickly using the appropriate tools. This section will help you and your students become more tech-savvy—by practicing with the tools that are already installed on your computers.

Simply go to the section pertaining to the type of project that you're interested in. The step-by-step instructions will get you well on your way to becoming a smooth operator—and your students too!

Coming Up Next:
- The Publisher
- The Presenter
- The Photographer
- The Producer

Execution

7. The Publisher

Have you ever wondered why some printed materials are effective—and others aren't?
Often the problem lies in the design, the realm of the publisher.

While the author has the primary responsibility for writing quality text, the *publisher* is responsible
for the overall quality of a finished print publication—like an article or a periodical, a pamphlet, a
newsletter, a book, or a Web page. The publisher's goal is to make a publication that

- leaves you with a lasting impression of the main idea,
- leads you to quickly survey the publication and retain the most significant details, and
- convinces you to do a more in-depth reading of the entire publication.

Techniques for creating a blueprint to an effective publication were discussed in the Design section
of this book under Global Design Principles and Blueprint Time. This section of the book focuses on
specific techniques to help your students execute their plans.

Desktop publishers use software specifically designed to create publications, such as cover pages,
newsletters, brochures, advertisements, signs, flyers, and catalogs. Microsoft Publisher is one of the most
popular desktop publishing applications. It has a multitude of features that will allow your students to
produce professional-quality designs. In addition, the program is loaded with templates that illustrate—
and give your students a head start on—a variety of common publications.

> **Teacher Tip:** On a Macintosh, I would recommend using Pages 1.01 to
> create magazine covers and newsletters. Pages can be ordered from the Mac
> online store (www.store.apple.com): from the home page, search for *iWork*.
> (Pages is included in iWork along with Keynote Speaker, which can be used
> instead of Microsoft PowerPoint, as described in The Presenter section.) For
> more detailed instructions on the software, use the site's Help feature.

Review the Introduction to Microsoft Publisher 2000 section that starts on the next page. Then choose
the type of publication you want to work on, from the Coming Up Next box below, and turn to that page
to learn how to put your students' plans into action.

Coming Up Next:
- Introduction to Microsoft Publisher 2000
- Creating a Cover Page
- Creating a Newsletter

Execution

Introduction to Microsoft Publisher 2000

On your PC, follow the steps below to get started in Microsoft Publisher:

Not Sure of Your Software Version? To see what version of Microsoft Publisher you are using, select the Publisher drop-down menu after the program opens and click on "About Publisher." A pop-up box showing the version number will appear. If you are using a different version of Microsoft Publisher than 2000 and are having trouble transferring these directions to your version, visit this Web site: http://office.microsoft.com/en-us/FX010857941033.aspx.

1. Open Microsoft Publisher by double-clicking on the icon.

2. Start a new publication.

   There are three different ways you and your students could begin making a publication. Each starting point has its own tab on the opening screen:

   - *Publications by Wizard* – This option takes you through a template process.

   - *Publications by Design* – This option offers sets of templates based on a similar theme or event.

   - *Blank Publications* – This option gives you a blank page to start a new publication from scratch.

Select the *Blank Publications* tab

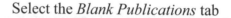

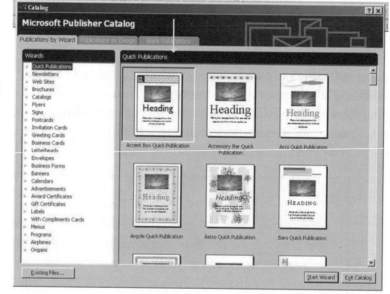

3. Select "Full Page" and click "Create."

   You will see a page like the one on the next page, with rulers and guides.

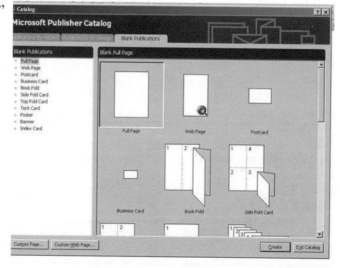

4. Establish the page parameters.

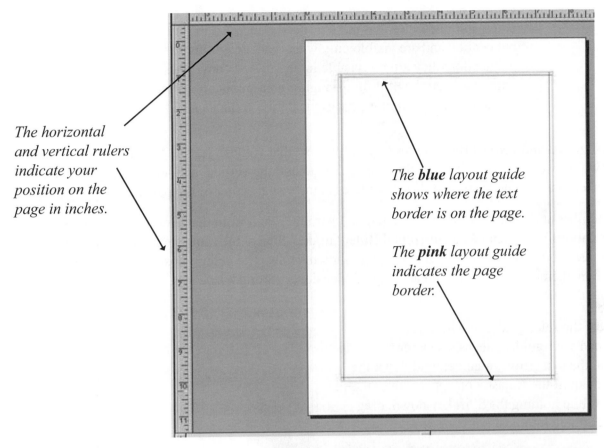

The horizontal and vertical rulers indicate your position on the page in inches.

*The **blue** layout guide shows where the text border is on the page.*

*The **pink** layout guide indicates the page border.*

At the top of your screen, you should see a toolbar, starting with "File."

Click on "Arrange," and from that drop-down menu, select "Layout Guides."

In this screen, enter the margins you want for your publication, as well as any column and row information.

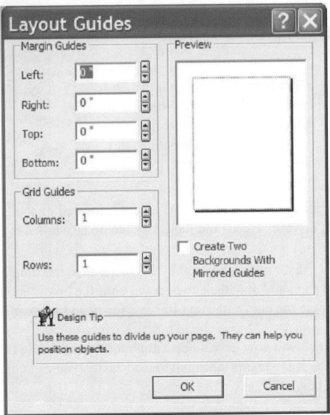

5. Identify the visual center of the page, using ruler guides.

> **Ruler guides**: Lines that mark a specific location in the publication and are visible only when you are editing the publication; they are not visible in the printed copy. These guides are very helpful for arranging your publications into quadrants and for lining up various items on the page.

Add horizontal and vertical ruler guides to your page so that you can see the location of the visual center while you are editing. Follow the steps below to add the vertical and horizontal golden means. Remember that the intersection of these two lines is the visual center of the page.

In the toolbar at the top of your screen, click on "Arrange," and from that drop-down menu, select "Ruler Guides" and then "Add Horizontal Ruler Guide." Repeat the same steps to add the vertical ruler guide. You'll see something like the page shown below. The default position of the ruler guides is at the mathematical midpoint of each page dimension, creating a *true center*. You must adjust them to create the *visual center*.

Positioning the Ruler Guides

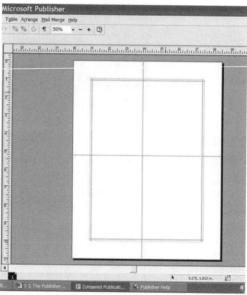

To adjust the ruler guides to where you've calculated your golden means, use your mouse to position the cursor over a guide; hold down the Shift key until the Adjust icon appears over the guide. While holding the Shift key down, drag the ruler guide into position.

6. Add text frames

> **Text frame**: An object in which you can add and edit written text. Once a text frame is created, you can edit its size, its position, and its font characteristics.

Begin by clicking on the text icon **A** located on the Drawing toolbar, which displays on the left of your screen (and looks like the image shown to the left here).

The cursor now appears as a $+$, rather than the standard arrow. To add the text frame, click on the page and drag the cursor down until the box is about the shape and size you wish. When you release the cursor, the text frame is ready and you can begin adding text.

Notice you now have a Formatting toolbar available to you for editing the appearance of the text. (If the text is too small to read easily, you can quickly enlarge the workspace by using the F9 key.)

7. Add picture frames.

> **Picture frame**: An object in which you can add and edit photographs or other graphics from your own files. Once a picture frame is created, you can edit its size, its position, and its coloring.

Begin by clicking on the appropriate icon located on the Drawing toolbar. If you wish to insert a photograph or image from your own files click on the ⊞ icon; if you wish to insert clip art, click on the ⊞ icon.

The cursor now appears as a $+$, rather than the standard arrow. To add the picture frame, click on the page and drag the cursor down until the box is about the shape and size you wish. When you release the cursor, the picture frame is ready and you can begin adding pictures by double-clicking on the picture frame. If you selected the Clip Organizer frame, the clip art menu will prompt you to select the appropriate clip art.

Notice you now have the Picture toolbar available to you for editing the appearance of the image.

> **Teacher Tip:** You can alter the coloring of images and clip art. Right-click on the object and select "Change Picture" and then "Recolor Picture." Select your desired coloring from the drop-down menu.

8. Add an appropriate background. In the toolbar at the top of your screen, click on "Format," and from that drop-down menu, select "Background" to choose from the options displayed there. You can also add other text and graphics, as described in the previous steps. Then select "Arrange" from the toolbar, then "Order" and "Send Backward" so that your foreground items are on top.

9. Resize and reposition frames. Once picture frames and text frames are created on the page, they can be easily resized and relocated by using simple drag-and-drop techniques.

Resize frames: To change the size of a frame and maintain its original proportions, click anywhere inside the frame until the frame has a black border and eight black squares appear at the corners and midpoints of the sides. These black squares are called *selection handles*. When you place the cursor over any of these selection handles, the resize operator appears. Click on one of the selection handles, and drag and drop RESIZE the frame to its new size.

> **Teacher Tip:**
> If you don't resize objects by using one of the *corner* selection handles, the frame will lose its original proportions!

Reposition frames: To change the location of a frame, click anywhere in the frame until the black border and selection handles appear. When you place the cursor over any part of the border lines *except* the selection handles; the relocate operator ⊹ MOVE appears. Click on the frame and drag and drop the frame to its new location.

Viewing the Final Product: To preview the final publication without boundaries and guides, simply go to "View" in the toolbar and uncheck "Boundaries and Guides."

Creating a Cover Page

Using the same steps and techniques you learned in the Introduction to Microsoft Publisher 2000 section, follow these more detailed steps to create a cover page:

1. Open Microsoft Publisher by double-clicking on the icon.

2. Start a new publication.

3. Select "Full Page" and click "Create."

4. Establish the page parameters. As a rule, cover pages do not have margins; if they did, there would be blank space all along the outside borders of the page. Modify the Layout Guides, setting all the margins to zero.

5. Identify the visual center of the page, using ruler guides. Remember, for a standard 8½" x 11" page, the horizontal golden mean is approximately 7" up from the bottom edge of the page, and the vertical golden mean is approximately 5½" from the right side of the page. Where these two lines intersect is the visual center of the page.

6. Add text frames. For your cover page, create a text frame for your *title block* and for your *teasers*.

7. Add picture frames.

8. Add an appropriate background.

9. Resize and reposition frames.

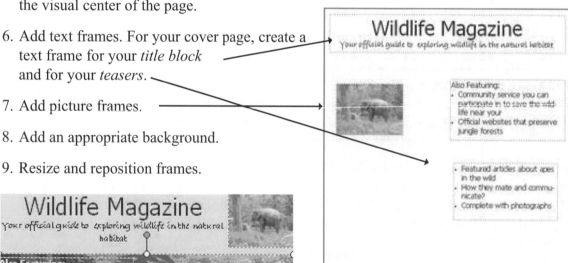

Notice how the elephant image has been reduced and moved to the title block. The teasers have also been moved and reformatted.

Creating a Newsletter

Using the same steps and techniques you learned in the Introduction to Microsoft Publisher 2000, follow these more detailed steps to create a newsletter:

Getting Started

1. Open Microsoft Publisher by double-clicking on the icon.

2. Start a new publication. Select "Full Page" and click "Create."

3. Establish the page parameters. Most newsletters have ½" margins on all sides, which creates a blank space all along the outside perimeter of the page. Newsletters are also usually designed with a four-column layout, with the left column usually containing teasers, a table of contents, and often an image. Modify the layout guides, setting all the margins to 0.5" and type "4" next to "Columns" under "Grid Guides."

4. Identify the visual center of the page, using ruler guides. Remember, for a standard 8½" x 11" page, the horizontal golden mean is approximately 7" up from the bottom edge of the page, and the vertical golden mean is approximately 5½" from the right side of the page. Where these two lines intersect is the visual center of the page.

5. Add text frames. For the front page of your newsletter, create text frames for your nameplate, articles, headlines, preview sections, and table of contents.

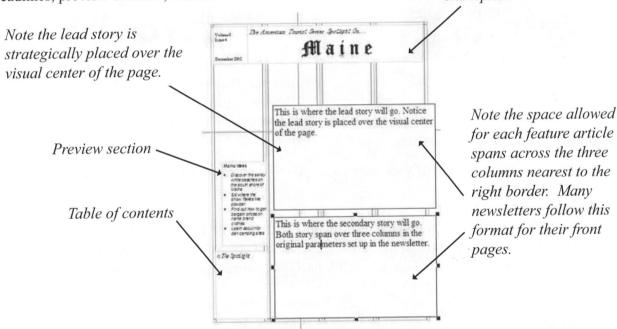

Note the lead story is strategically placed over the visual center of the page.

Nameplate

Preview section

Table of contents

Note the space allowed for each feature article spans across the three columns nearest to the right border. Many newsletters follow this format for their front pages.

Setting the Tone: Front Page

Font types and colors schemes, especially those of the nameplate, are the most influential components of a newsletter's visual appearance and tone. These visual characteristics are critical because they give the reader an instant impression of the document and influence the reader's first reaction to the newsletter.

Formatting the Nameplate

The nameplate is a very stylistic component of a publication. It is located in a prominent position on the cover page, and it sets the tone of the newsletter as well as of the organization that publishes it. Therefore, the color scheme, font style, logo, and slogans of the nameplate, and the rest of the cover page, must be consistent with the impression you want to portray.

The nameplate should contain the title (in a large, bold font), publication date, volume and issue numbers, and identifier of the publishing organization (e.g., logo, slogan, or icon).

The font used in your title, as well as the other fonts used on the front page, is one of the first and most telling features of your newsletter and contributes significantly to the overall tone of the publication. Notice in the image below, the *American Tourist* organization uses an italicized Informal Roman font to introduce the different issues in their series. This font portrays a smart and sophisticated look that is appropriate for a travel series. For this edition that features Maine, an Old English font is used to give "Maine" a historic and classic appearance. Notice how these two types of fonts work together to establish the overall tone of the publication.

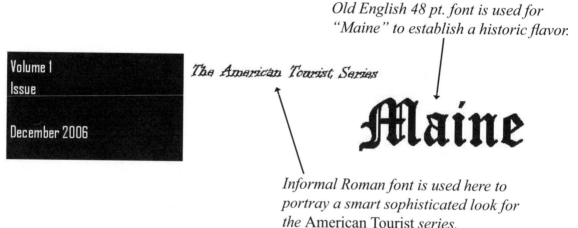

Old English 48 pt. font is used for "Maine" to establish a historic flavor.

Informal Roman font is used here to portray a smart sophisticated look for the American Tourist *series.*

Formatting the Front Page Articles

In the remaining three columns of your front page, you will place your important articles.

Article Placement and Layout

The *lead article* gets the most prominent position on the front page of a newsletter because it is the most significant. It is located on or around the visual center, and it straddles the columns of the article. The headline of the article usually contains powerful, intriguing words that grab the reader's attention.

Formatting Newsletter Articles

Newsletter articles are written in columns rather than page-width paragraphs. The shorter lines allow readers to scan the articles quickly without losing their place when beginning each new line.

Another tool publishers use to make the columns easier to read quickly is full justification. When text is fully justified, the left and right margins of each column have straight edges that leave a consistent space between columns and give readers' eyes exact starting and ending points on each line.

Font choice can also be a significant aid to readers. As you learned in the Design section, a serif font is much easier to read for bodies of text, such as a newsletter article, than a sans serif font.

Using the techniques you have learned so far, follow these steps to add text frames for all your articles. The only characteristics that may change from article to article are the location on the page and the size of the text frame, depending on the length of the article.

1. Add the text frame for your article.

2. Format the text frame. The lead article should span three columns and about half the page length. In the "Text Frame Properties" dialogue box, set the number of columns to "3."

3. Format the font and alignment of the text frame. Use the formatting tool bar to select a serif font size and type appropriate for the article and to select full justification for the alignment.

4. Add another text frame inside the article's text frame for the article's headline. Format the headline frame with a bold font no smaller than 14 pt. The headline's text frame should be located at the top left corner of the article text frame—not centered!

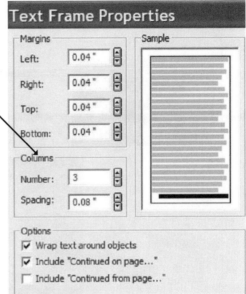

5. Add colors to the text frames. Click on the text frame to select the text frame you wish to fill with color. Be sure the selected text frame has the eight selection handles displayed and right-click on the frame. The "Format Text Box" dialogue box will appear. Select "Fill Color" and "More Colors" to select the color you want.

> **Teacher Tip:** You can preview a publication in different color schemes by selecting "Task Pane" under the "View" menu. Then choose "Color Schemes" from the drop-down menu. For more information about choosing color schemes, read the note on page 135.

6. Add picture frames. A great place to find pictures for your students' newsletters is www.pics4learning.com.

7. Format frame borders. When you create text frames, a black border line appears along the perimeter of the text frame by default. For a newsletter article, you will want to remove this border so that the article will blend into the page; this provides a more professional and unified appearance. To remove text frame borders follow these steps: Select the text box and right-click on it. Select "Change Frame" and then "Line Border Style"; choose "None."

8. Add accent lines. Adding accent lines gives the newsletter a clean look, separating articles and objects from one another. Experiment with accent lines in your own publications; they can contribute to a good layout by providing division and boundaries, but they can also clutter the page if overused. To insert an accent line on your newsletter, click on the "Line Tool" ＼ located on the Drawing toolbar.

The cursor now appears as a ＋ rather than the standard arrow. To add the line, click on the spot where you want the line to begin and drag the cursor until the line is the desired length. When you release the cursor, the line appears on the publication.

Teacher Tip: Hold down the Shift key while drawing a line to create a perfectly straight line. You can also add color or effects to your accent lines to complement the color scheme. To do this, right-click on the line and select "Change Line." From there, you can change the line color and line style, and add effects like a shadow.

Volume 1
Issue

December 2006

The American Tourist Series

Maine

Main Ideas

* Discover the sandy white beaches on the south shore of Maine.

* Ski where the snow flakes like powder.

* Find out how to get bargain prices on name brand clothes.

* Learn about hidden sales.

In The Spotlight:

Visit Maine's Breathtaking Coastlines

This is where the lead story should be written. The lead story should be about 200 words. Notice the title of the lead story is placed over the visual center of the page. The title of the lead story also spans two columns. This is where the lead story should be written.

This is where the lead story should be written. The lead story should be about 200 words. Notice the title of the lead story is placed over the visual center

of the page. The title of the lead story also spans two columns. This is where the lead story should be written.

This is where the lead story should be written. The lead story should be about 200 words. Notice the title of the lead story is placed over the visual center of the page. The title of the lead story also spans two columns. This is where the lead story should be written.

This is where the lead story should be

written. The lead story should be about 200 words. Notice the title of the lead story is placed over the visual center of the page. The title of the lead story also spans two columns. This is where the lead story should be written.

This is where the lead story should be written. The lead story should be about 200 words. Notice the title of the lead story is placed over the visual center of the page. The title of the lead story also spans two columns. This is where the lead story should be written.

Maine Ski Resorts Second to None

This is where the secondary story should be written. Many times it is the second most interesting article in the newsletter.

This is where the secondary story should be written. Many times it is the

second most interesting article in the newsletter.

This is where the secondary story should be written. Many times it is the second most interesting article in the newsletter.

This is where the secondary story should be written. Many times it is the

second most interesting article in the newsletter.

This is where the secondary story should be written. Many times it is the second most interesting article in the newsletter.

Formatting the Table of Contents

Newsletters typically have a table of contents on the front page so the reader can quickly identify and locate articles of personal interest and regular features of the newsletter. A professional-looking table of contents has dots, called a dot *leader*, to assist the reader in locating the page number of the articles. Follow the steps below to create and format a table of contents:

Tab ruler

1. Add a text frame for the table of contents.

2. Set the tab stop for the page numbers. Double-click on the tab ruler where you want the page numbers to appear in your text frame. The "Tabs" dialogue box will appear.

3. Format the tab leaders. Select "Right" Alignment and "Dot" Leader; then click "OK."

4. Add the entries. Type the text into the table of contents text frame. After each entry hit the Tab key. Microsoft Publisher automatically adds the dot leaders. Then type the corresponding page number.

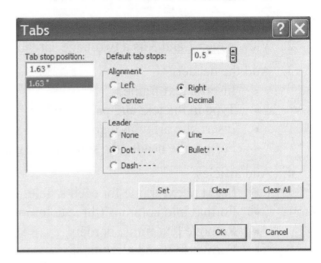

A Note about Color Schemes

A good color scheme is important to the newsletter's impact. Review the effects of some basic color relationships in the Global Design Principles section (see p. 96), so you can help your students make effective choices.

When selecting colors for components of a newsletter, keep in mind the following techniques:

- Use contrast between the font color and the fill color on the nameplate and other colored text frames, so that the words stand out.

- Select colors that augment the colors appearing in the photographs and graphics in the newsletter.

- Do not overwhelm the newsletter with too many competing colors. Maintain uniformity throughout the publication by using a continuous color scheme. Make sure students don't use more than four colors.

- Choose a color scheme in advance and maintain it throughout the entire newsletter.

Inside Pages

In most four-page newsletters, the inside two pages are printed on the same side of a larger piece of paper, separated by a fold down the middle. In this next section, you will examine techniques for designing a two-page spread for the inside of a newsletter. For the inside pages, you will have several articles accompanied by pull quotes or photographs.

Below is a checklist of all the steps required to add the inside pages to your four-page newsletter:

1. Insert two new pages.
2. View pages 2 and 3 as a two-page spread.
3. Add the header.
   - Insert a text frame.
   - Type in the text and page number.
   - Insert clip art with logo.
   - Format the header the same as the nameplate.
4. Add articles.
   - Insert a text frame for each article.
   - Format into columns (three columns for the lead article).
   - Remove text frame borders.
   - Format font and alignment.
   - Insert a text frame for the headline.
   - Format the headline font.
5. Add visual expression to complement the articles.
   - Insert picture frames or clip art.
6. Add pull quotes to complement the articles.
   - Insert text frames.
   - Format the text.
7. Add accent lines wherever needed to complement the style and tone of the newsletter.

Insert New Pages

Select "Insert" from the top toolbar, then "Page." The "Insert Page" dialogue box appears. To insert two pages, enter "2" next to "Number of new pages" and click "OK."

View Inside Pages as a Spread

Select "View" from the top toolbar, then "Two-Page Spread." Notice the status bar at the bottom of the screen now contains page navigation tools.

Page navigation tools

You can move from page to page of your newsletter by selecting the appropriate page number on the page navigation tool. You should see both pages together, as shown in the image on the opposite page.

Two-Page Spread

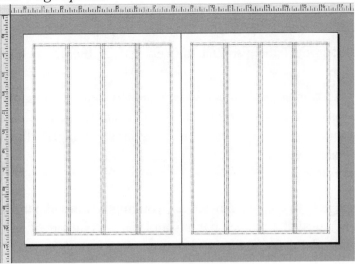

Back Page

Next you will add the back page of your newsletter. Follow the steps on the checklist below to add and format the back page of your newsletter. For the back page, you probably want to have three sections, containing the following information:

- Section 1: the group's logo, the group name and all of the group members' names
- Section 2: the school name, teacher name, course title, and period number
- Section 3: a feature containing light, witty, and humorous facts about the main topic

Sample back page

Below is a checklist of all the steps required to create the back page of our newsletter:

1. Insert a new page.

2. Insert and format three text frames.

3. Insert clip art with the logo in the Section 1.

4. Add back page features.
   - Insert text frame for article.
   - Remove text frame borders.
   - Format font and alignment.

5. Add visual expression to complement the articles.
   - Insert a picture frame or clip art in Section 3.

6. Add accent lines wherever needed to complement the style and tone of the newsletter.

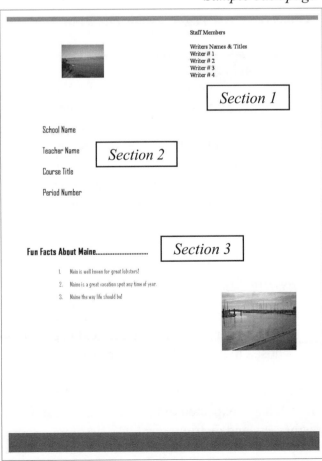

> **Teacher Tip:** The checklists provided on the previous pages can serve two purposes:
>
> 1. You can easily reproduce them so that students can use them to help create their newsletters.
>
> 2. You can also you them as assessment and evaluation tools. You may also want to add a content-based checklist or rubric that explains to students what content you are expecting to see in the project. Their final grade should comprise the two grades: the content and the technical.

Now that you have learned how to create a newsletter, you might want take this a step further and create an online classroom newsletter to keep parents and students informed on your daily homework assignments, classroom calendar dates, and other important happenings in your classroom.

In his 1989 book *Easy Ways to Make Technology Work for You,* Dr. Dockterman suggests using the following Web sites to create an online classroom newsletter:

- Scholastic's Class Homepage Builder – teacherscholastic.com/homepagebuilder
- Placemark (Tom Snyder Productions) – placemark.tomsnyder.com/placemark
- Education Planet's Teacher Web Tools – www.teacherwebtools.com
- MySchoolonline – www.myschoolonline.com
- McGraw-Hill Learning Network – mhln.com
- Quia.com Class Pages – www.quia.com

> **Teacher Tip:**
> You have software options other than Microsoft Publisher available to you. You can access CNet at www.download.com for the teaching tools in education. Use the search box to find Printmaster Express 15.0. You can access a trial version of this software and then purchase it for only $9.99 if you are happy with it. You also may want to try Neobook Professional Multimedia 5.0, which offers a 30-day free trial as well. You should try any software product out at home before sharing it with your classes. You can also access tutorials from the company's Web pages, using the Help option.

Assessing Student Progress

Your students are finally at the end of the Execution phase of their projects. It is now time to formally evaluate their performance. On the next page is a rubric for you to use when assessing students who have chosen to be "Publishers" for their projects.

Remember, it can be helpful for students to have this information at the beginning of the lesson so they know what is expected of them. For that reason, the rubric is provided as a separate page that you can easily copy and distribute.

Rubric: The Publisher

The following rubric will be used to evaluate your final project, your knowledge entity.

The library media specialist may be in charge of assessing this section of your project.

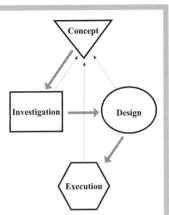

	Not Yet	*Okay*	*Excellent*
Concept	The publication is not indicative of the concept. It appears that little or no time was spent prewriting and analyzing the concept.	The publication represents the concept, but it does not demonstrate that you came to a deeper understanding of the concept. It appears that minimal time was spent prewriting and analyzing the concept.	The publication is indicative of the concept and clearly demonstrates that you came to a deeper understanding of the concept. It appears that a lot of time was spent prewriting and analyzing the concept.
Investigation *(see above)*	The publication does not demonstrate results from your investigation. There is little or no information gathered. Information is not organized or authenticated.	The publication demonstrates that you did minimal investigation. There is some information gathered. The information is organized but not authenticated.	The publication demonstrates that you did extensive investigation. There is a lot of information gathered. The information is organized by virtual index cards, and all information was authenticated.
Design	The publication does not follow your design. Your design does not follow the Global Design Principles.	The publication reflects your original design and follows some of the Global Design Principles.	The publication's execution caused your original design to change for the better. Your publication reflects the Global Design Principles.
Execution	The publication shows no creativity and is not fully executed.	The publication is fully executed. It represents the concept, but lacks in true ingenuity.	The publication shows your unique talents and creativity: it could only have been created by you. You went beyond the scope of the book and found other tips to help you create your publication.

8. The Presenter

Have you ever wondered how your teachers know what to say and what audiovisual aids to use in class? They're using the presenter skills they've learned.

The *presenter* delivers a main idea to a live audience. A good presenter know his subject matter inside and out. But just as important, a good presenter presents that subject matter in a simple and concise manner, highlighting the most important points and explaining them in detail. Although the presenter does the majority, if not all, of the talking, a good presentation is interactive. A powerful presenter uses multimedia tools to involve the audience members and encourage their participation.

The speech and multimedia objects work together to highlight the most significant points in the presentation. A dynamic presenter might accompany the spoken part of the presentation with handouts, slide shows, illustrations on white boards or flip charts, audio clips, video clips, animations, models, artwork, or other objects that can emphasize the topic with their touch, taste, or smell. In addition to highlighting the most significant points of the presentation, these multimedia objects grab and keep the audience's interest.

Presenters need to be tech-savvy to create a dynamic presentation with audio clips, video clips, animations, models, artwork, or other objects. Microsoft PowerPoint is one of the most popular presentation applications available today. PowerPoint is specifically designed for creating presentations and has a multitude of features that allow users to produce professional-quality presentations.

> **Teacher Tip:** If you are using a Macintosh, you may want to use Keynote Speaker 2 instead of Microsoft PowerPoint. It is a great presentation tool that is available through Apple's iWork software package. To try the program, go to www.store.apple.com and search for *iWork*. There are great tutorials for Keynote Speaker through the Help menu. Select "Start new project" and use the Help menu to guide you through the creation of your slides.
>
> Whatever software you decide to use, don't forget to use the tips in this section to create and deliver a successful presentation.

This chapter helps you apply the techniques you learned in the Global Design Principles section. Your students can use their outlines, as described in the Blueprint Time section, and your instructions from this section to put together their class presentations.

Coming Up Next:
- Creating Presentations in Microsoft PowerPoint 2004
- Delivering Effective Presentations

Execution

Creating Presentations in Microsoft PowerPoint 2004

On your PC or Mac, follow the steps below to get started in Microsoft PowerPoint.

Note: In this section, the screen shots are from a Mac but the directions can easily be transferred to your PC.

> **Not Sure of Your Software Version?** To see what version of Microsoft PowerPoint you are using, select the PowerPoint drop-down menu after the program opens and click on "About PowerPoint." A pop-up box showing the version number will appear. If you are using a different version of Microsoft PowerPoint than 2004 and are having trouble transferring these directions to your version, visit this Web site: http://www.microsoft.com/smallbusiness/tips/powerpoint-tips.mspx.

1. Open Microsoft PowerPoint by double-clicking on the icon.

2. Start a new publication.

There are two different ways you and your students could begin making a publication. Each starting point has its own tab on the opening screen: Each starting point can be selected from the formatting palette on the side of the screen under "Change Slides."
   - *Presentations Starting with a Template* – This option starts you with a structured template.
   - *Blank Presentations* – This option gives you a blank page to start a new presentation from scratch.

3. Select "Add Blank Slide" under "Add Objects."

It is better to use a blank slide rather than a pre-designed template. It gives you more creative freedom to design your project to better suit the needs of your topic. Lynell Burmark summarizes her sentiments on using templates:

"I would be remiss not to mention one more freebie that comes with most presentation software: pre-designed templates, complete with color suggestions and graphical elements. 'Yes, your presentation can look like those of thousands of other professionals,' these all-too convenient templates want you to believe. The risk is that your audience will fall asleep, comfortably assuming they've seen it all before." (Burmark, 2002, p. 77)

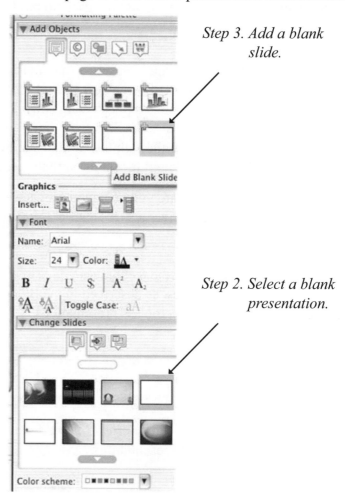

Step 3. Add a blank slide.

Step 2. Select a blank presentation.

Working with Text

Creating Text Frames

To add text to a presentation, you need to create a text frame. Once a text frame is created, you can edit its size, position, and font characteristics. For example, for your first slide you'll want to create a text frame for the title.

1. Begin by clicking on the [icon] icon located on the Drawing toolbar. The cursor now appears as a $+$.

2. To add the text frame, click on the presentation and drag the cursor down until the box is the shape and size you wish. When you release the cursor, the text frame is ready and you can begin adding text.

Notice you now have a Formatting toolbar available to you for editing the appearance of the text.

(If the text is too small to read easily, you can enlarge it with the options in your Formatting toolbar. Remember to refer to the Global Design Principles to decide what type of font to use in your presentation.)

How Much Text Is Too Much?

Text box on title slide

Lynell Burmark gives us a good rule of thumb when adding text to your slides. She suggests the rule of 6 x 6: "No more than six words across and no more than six lines down." With this in mind, Burmark suggests fonts no smaller than 24 points. She advocates for using more pictures than text in presentations, saying that 90% of her slide shows are pictures, so she has an opportunity to share her personal stories and shared experiences and to interact with the audience. (Burmark, 2002, p. 72)

> Our Trip to the
> Bronx Zoo

Using Colors Wisely

When selecting colors for components of the presentation, bear in mind some of the following pointers:

- Use contrast between the font color and the fill color, so the words stand out.
- Select colors that augment colors in the graphics that appear throughout the presentation.
- Do not overwhelm the audience with too many competing colors.
- Choose a color scheme and format in advance and maintain it throughout the entire presentation.
- Lynell Burmark suggests blue for the background color of the slide. She says, "it's restful and calming and evokes images of pleasant natural elements such as water and sky." (p. 42)
- Burmark also suggests using yellow for text and highlighting. "Of all the 16.7 million colors the human eye can see, it will go to yellow first" (pp. 73–74).
- Burmark states that red is also a good attention-getting color.

The color scheme should be planned out before designing the presentation. Review the effects of some basic color relationships in the Global Design Principles section (see p. 96).

In PowerPoint, you have the option to use one of its prepared color schemes. On the Formatting palette under the slides, you will see a drop-down menu for "Color Scheme." Before selecting your color scheme from these choices, make sure you understand how they work:

Prepared color schemes

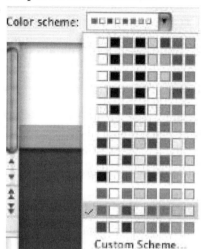

- The first color is the background color for the slide.

- The second color is the primary text and line color.

- The third color is the shadows scheme color.

- The sixth color is the hyperlink color.

- The other colors in the color scheme palette are seldom used.

Your students can also create a custom color scheme to demonstrate their creativity. You may want to insist on this as part of your students' assignment. (The custom option is at the bottom of the scheme list.)

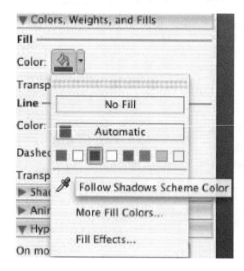

Adding Color to a Text Frame

1. Select the text frame by clicking on it. Be sure the selection handles are displayed.
2. Use the Formatting palette and select "Colors," "Weights," and "Fills."
3. Select the paint brush icon; a drop-down menu of colors will appear.
4. Select the color you want for the background of the text box.

> Instead of using the Formatting palette to add color to a text box, you can right-click on the text box.

Working with Pictures

Creating Picture Frames

To add a picture to a presentation, you need to create a picture frame. Once a picture frame is created, you can edit its size, position, and coloring.

1. Begin by clicking on the appropriate icon located on the Drawing toolbar. If you wish to insert a photograph or image from your own files click on the ⊞ icon; if you wish to insert clip art, click on the ⊞ icon. The cursor now appears as a +, rather than the standard arrow.

2. To add the picture frame, click on the page and drag the cursor down until the box is about the shape and size you wish. When you release the cursor, the picture frame is ready and you can begin adding pictures by double-clicking on the picture frame. If you selected the Clip Art Gallery tool, the menu will prompt you to select the appropriate clip art.

Notice you now have the Picture toolbar available to you for editing the appearance of the image.

A word about clip art: It is imperative that students are not allowed to turn in clip art as part of their "original" work. It "deprives them of the synergistic access to both sides of their brain (drawing images from the right side of the brain, drawing words from the left.) Meltzer provides a helpful comparison in the table below" (Burmark, 2002, p. 13).

Use of Original Artwork	Use of Clip Art
Ownership of work	No ownership of work
Growth	No growth
Self-expression	No self-expression
Acceptance of student's work	Unintended criticism of student
Gain in self-confidence	No gain in self-confidence
Learn observation skills	No observation skills learned
Learn more computer skills	Learn fewer computer skills
Unique products	Canned look
Cohesive style	Possible mishmash of styles
Creative experience	Not a creative experience
Extensive decision making	Minimal decision making

Editing Pictures

To edit or add special effects to the pictures, use the "Effects" icon in the Picture toolbar. For example, think about how recoloring a picture in black and white or in grayscale could change the tone and mood of your publication.

Study the pictures below. Decide which effect would be better for a particular message.

Fully colored picture with no special effects

Picture with graphic pen, right diagonal stroke

Picture with ripple effect

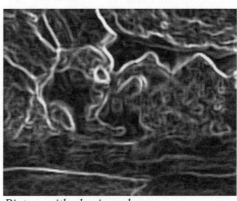

Picture with glowing edges

Working with Sound

Sound in presentations is often overlooked, but it can have a huge impact.

Getting high-quality sound into your presentation is a fairly easy process. PowerPoint is equipped with many prerecorded sounds that are readily available to you with a click of a button. It is also easy to import sound into your computer. It usually involves using a microphone or a CD; today it is also easy to download music from the Internet.

Sound is usually successful when it is used to thoughtfully complement visuals on the screen. This technique creates a more meaningful and powerful experience for the audience.

Below are a few pointers for incorporating different types of sound in your presentation:

- **Voice** can be used in your presentation by connecting a microphone to your computer. Although this is a great feature, it should be used sparingly. The audience is much more likely to enjoy a live presentation than a recording of your voice.

- **Music** can be a great addition to your presentation. You can copy music from a CD in your computer's CD drive, download a song from the Internet, or, better yet, compose your own song. If you are using someone else's music, please be sure to ask your teacher or library media specialist about copyright laws. I strongly suggest avoiding copyright issues by having students compose their own songs with readily available software programs such as Garage Band.

- **Other sounds** can be incorporated. Many programs have sounds included in their software packages. Placed appropriately, these sounds can enhance a presentation. Students have a tendency to overuse these sounds, randomly placing them throughout the presentation so that they become distracting. Examples of appropriate use of sounds are to transition between slides and to emphasize a point or highlight a particular topic.

Adding Sounds

Follow the steps below to add sound to your presentation. Use the pointers and skills discussed so far.

1. Decide on the type of sound that should be added to the presentation.

2. Select "Insert" from the menu at the top of the screen.

3. Select "Movies and Sounds."

4. Select the source of the sound.

5. Incorporate the sound into your presentation.

6. Decide when the sound should play. (At the beginning of the slide? Or when you select a button on your slide?) Right-click on the [icon] icon to view the Sound Options.

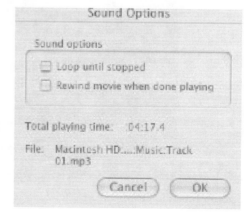

Using PowerPoint Sounds

Follow the steps below to incorporate PowerPoint's prerecorded sounds into your presentation:

1. Select "Slide Show" and then "Custom Animation." A pop-up menu will appear. In the first box to the right where it says "Select to Animate," a list of the different elements on your slide appears.

2. Highlight the appropriate component of the slide that you want animated in your presentation.

3. Use the "Effect Options" button on the left of the screen to add the sound to the slide.

Working with Graphs and Charts

Most people are better at remembering pictures than bunches of numbers. Graphs and charts are a great way to take numbers and make them into pictures.

Students should begin graphing and using charts at an early age in school. This simple exercise is a great one for first graders. Bring in bags of M&Ms and have the students predict how many candies of each color are included in the bags. Then break the students into groups of four, where they sort the colors. Each student in the group then graphs one color on a "Final Results Graph." This graph can be shared with the rest of the class and compared to the original predictions.

At the secondary level, graphing should be introduced to students on a more sophisticated level, especially in their math and science classes. In physics, students might be asked to graph the distance an object falls with its velocity. Graphing is also applicable to social studies and language arts classrooms. In a social studies classroom, students could graph on a pie chart who was to blame for causing the French Revolution. In a language arts classroom, students could use a pie chart to determine who is to blame for Caesar's death in Shakespeare's play *Julius Caesar*. As students begin using graphs and charts in more of their classes, they will begin to understand how graphs are pictures that represent numbers.

Choosing the Appropriate Graph

Students are often tempted to select the "coolest" graph available to them—rather than the most appropriate. The information in the table below can help students identify the appropriate graphs for their presentations. In addition, Microsoft Office, in its Help feature, provides "Examples of Chart Types," which explains the different types of graphs along with a visual representation of each one. Students should take a few moments and browse through the Help feature to get a better idea of some of the differences between the graphs. The most common graphs are listed below:

Chart Types

Type	Appropriate Use
Column	• To shows data changes over a period of time • To illustrate a comparison among items
Bar	• To compare individual items • To compare values, with less emphasis on time (categories are organized vertically, values horizontally)
Line	• To show trends in data at equal intervals
Pie	• To compare the size of individual items to the sum of those items • To emphasize a significant event

Keep in mind, when students include graphs in their presentations, it is imperative that they not only know which type of graphs to use, but also how to discuss and present the graphs.

Adding Graphs and Charts to a Presentation

Follow the steps below to add a graph to your presentation:

1. Select "Insert" from the menu at the top of the screen.

2. Select "Chart." A graph appears with an Excel spreadsheet behind it. Select the Excel spreadsheet to input the numbers you want graphed. Delete any columns you don't need. Label each column appropriately for your data series.*

			A	B	C	D
			1st Qtr	2nd Qtr	3rd Qtr	4th Qtr
1		East	20.4	27.4	90	20.4
2		West	30.6	38.6	34.6	31.6
3		North	45.9	46.9	45	43.9

Graph in ourtriptotheza

3. Highlight your new data series. Click on the graphing icon and select the appropriate graph.

4. Your new graph is now incorporated into your presentation.

5. Animate your graph in preparation for presentation. In normal view, select the "Slide Show" menu and click "Custom Animation." In the dialogue box, click the chart and then "Add Effect." Select an effect from the pop-up dialogue box. Select "OK." Set the visible options (e.g, Start, Direction, and Speed).

6. Click on "Effect Options" for the effect you added. Select "Chart Animation" in the dialogue box. Next to "Group Chart," select one of the following options and then click "OK" (depending on the chart type, not all options may be available):

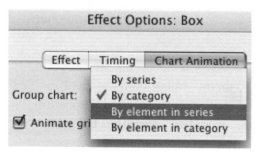

- As one object – the entire chart will appear
- By series – each series will appear by itself
- By category – each category will appear as an object

*Note: *Series* and *categories* are rows and columns from your database.

Delivering Effective Presentations

One of the most important aspects of the presentation is the actual live presentation of the material. You need to carefully plan ways to entice your audience and to interact with them. Successful presenters plan questions and discussion activities for their audiences before they begin their actual presentations. They also practice the presentations—before presentation day.

Many successful presenters will begin their presentations with a teaser. A good way to get the audience involved is to begin with a few questions on a slide. Provide the audience two minutes of think time. Then move to the next slide, which is blank, and prompt the audience to respond to the questions. Record their responses on the blank slide before actually beginning the presentation.

Another technique many presenters use is to create an Action Items list as they present. During a presentation, the audience may come up with good ideas. During the presentation, you can record all the good ideas shared by your classmates. Then, after the presentation, you will have a list to share with the class.

Remember to share all of these tips with your students, so they can become effective presenters, too!

Presentation Tools

Review the PowerPoint tool descriptions below to enhance your presenting skills.

Using Meeting Minutes and Action Items

To access Meeting Minutes and Action Items, you must be in presentation mode. The presentation mode icon is located on the bottom left of your PowerPoint screen.

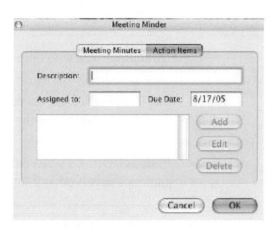

1. Right-click on the presentation screen and select "Meeting Minder." A pop-up menu appears.

2. Select "Meeting Minutes" if you want to take a few notes during the presentation or "Action Items" to develop a To Do list.

   In Action Items, your classmates are forced to take ownership of the item they want completed because it prompts you for the responsible party and a due date. It is a great way to get things done with a large group.

Using Pointer Options

To access Pointer Options, such as the presentation pen, you must be in presentation mode. Again, the mode icons are located on the bottom left of your PowerPoint screen.

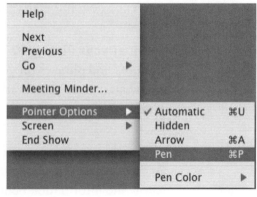

1. Right-click on the presentation screen and select "Pointer Options." (If you have a Mac and don't have a two-button mouse, hold the Ctrl key while you click.) A pop-up menu appears.

2. Select "Pen." (If you want to change the color of the pen, select "Pen Color.")

Your cursor now changes into a pen, so you can circle things for emphasis on your screen during the presentation—like this bear's face as he plays in the water at the zoo.

Example of using the presentation pen to highlight information during a presentation

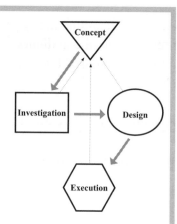

E-1 Delivering Your Presentation

Remember this: The more presentations you do, the better you'll get at them.

It is easy to get excited about your presentation and maybe even overwhelmed by all of this technology, but the best technique is to pace yourself. Practice your presentation ahead of time, so you know the material inside and out.

Use the guidelines below to help you perfect your presenting techniques:

- **Pace yourself.** Don't speak so quickly that the audience doesn't have time to digest and understand the material.

- **Plan activities.** Have some activities and questions planned to get your audience involved and interacting with the material.

- **Provide wait time.** *Wait time* is silence. Enduring a little silence while your audience views the slides before you begin talking lets them attach more meaning to the slides.

- **Use Meeting Minders.** This tool is a great way to track notes and create a To Do list while presenting your material. It is a good way to demonstrate to your audience how imperative their input is to the success of your presentation.

- **Look at your audience.** You should know your material inside and out. The pictures and phrases on your slides should prompt your talking while you look at the audience. You should not spend your entire presentation reading off the slides.

- **Practice, practice, practice!** Practicing your presentation in front of a mirror or in front of other classmates will make you a better speaker. It will help you know the information better and help you get your pacing and voice inflections down pat.

Distribute Handout E-1 as a handy reminder for students preparing to give their presentations.

Assessing Student Progress

Your students are finally at the end of the Execution phase of their projects. It is now time to formally evaluate their performance. On the next page is a rubric for you to use when assessing students who have chosen to be "Presenters" for their projects.

Remember, it can be helpful for students to have this information at the beginning of the lesson so they know what is expected of them. For that reason, the rubric is provided as a separate page that you can easily copy and distribute.

Rubric: The Presenter

The following rubric will be used to evaluate your final project, your knowledge entity.

The library media specialist may be in charge of assessing this section of your project.

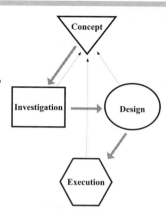

Phase	Not Yet	Okay	Excellent
Concept	The presentation is not indicative of the concept. It appears that little or no time was spent prewriting and analyzing the concept.	The presentation represents the concept, but it does not demonstrate that you came to a deeper understanding of the concept. It appears that minimal time was spent prewriting and analyzing the concept.	The presentation is indicative of the concept and clearly demonstrates that you came to a deeper understanding of the concept. It appears that a lot of time was spent prewriting and analyzing the concept.
Investigation *(see above)*	The presentation does not demonstrate results from your investigation. There is little or no information gathered. Information is not organized or authenticated.	The presentation demonstrates that you did minimal investigation. There is some information gathered. The information is organized but not authenticated.	The presentation demonstrates that you did extensive investigation. There is a lot of information gathered. The information is organized by virtual index cards, and all information was authenticated.
Design	The presentation does not follow your design. Your design does not follow the Global Design Principles and does not adhere to the 6 words per bullet rule.	The presentation reflects your original design and follows some of the Global Design Principles. The presentation does adhere to the 6 words per bullet rule.	The presentation's execution caused your original design to change for the better. Your presentation reflects the Global Design Principles and adheres to the 6 words per bullet rule.
Execution	The presentation shows no creativity and is not fully executed. Slides are read to the audience directly from the screen.	The presentation is fully executed. It represents the concept, but lacks in true ingenuity. Slides are not read to the audience, but the audience is not engaged in the presentation.	The presentation shows your unique talents and creativity: it could only have been created by you. You went beyond the scope of the book and found other tips to help you create your presentation. You know your material inside and out, and you engage the audience by using Meeting Minutes and questions.

9. The Photographer

Pictures are a great way to share an experience, a moment in time, or a place with your viewers. They are a great addition to any publication, presentation, or movie. Photographs spice up and personalize your projects. Sometime photographers take a number of pictures about a certain topic or time period that they then arrange into a slide show, to make a statement of some sort.

To help them with this task, photographers use software designed specifically to help them edit, store, organize, and share their photos.

One of those programs is iPhoto, a program that is specifically designed for and simplifies the entire process. It allows you to import pictures from different sources—for example, a digital camera, hard drive, CD—and then helps you organize the pictures. Then it allows you to easily share those pictures with other viewers, in a variety of formats.

iPhoto even has a special editing tool that can be used to touch up your photographs.

> **Teacher Tip:** If you are using a PC or don't have access to iPhoto, you may want to use www.picaboo.com—where you can download free photo software. The software has the same sort of interface as iPhoto, so the directions in this section will still apply. PhotoJam is another program like iPhoto and can be downloaded from www.shockwave.com/sw/content/photojam. Another great free download for PC users is Picasa; it can be accessed at http://picasa.google.com/index.html.
>
> For slide shows with no music, you may want to visit www.snapfish.com.

This chapter will help you and your students learn how to work with your photographs. This will enable your students to show off the photography techniques they learned from the Design section of this book.

Jim Heid in his book, *The Macintosh iLife,* includes Tips for Better Digital Photography, which are included on Handout E-2 (p. 160). Distribute this handout to your students, so they can refer to his advice, as well as to the photography tips included in the Design section.

You and your students will be expert photographers in no time.

Coming Up Next:
- Preparing Your Pictures with iPhoto 6
- Sharing Your Pictures

Execution

Preparing Your Pictures with iPhoto 6

Follow the steps below to get started in iPhoto on your Macintosh computer.

Not Sure of Your Software Version? To see what version of iPhoto you are using, select the iPhoto drop-down menu after the program opens and click on "About iPhoto." A pop-up box showing the version number will appear. If you are using a different version of Microsoft iPhoto and are having trouble transferring these directions to your version, visit this Web site: http://www.apple.com/support/iphoto.

Importing Pictures into iPhoto

Importing from a Digital Camera

1. Open iPhoto by double-clicking on the icon, which is usually on the bottom menu bar on the Mac.

2. Connect your digital camera to a USB port on your Mac. (The USB ports are usually located under the keyboard.)

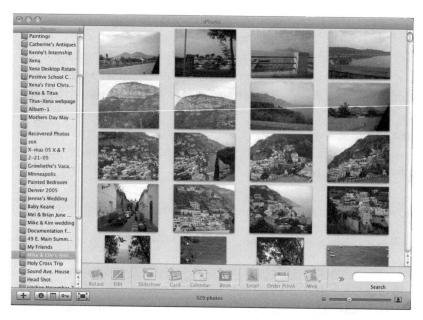

3. Turn the camera on and set the mode switch on the camera to playback mode. (The button usually looks like an arrow on the digital camera.)

4. Once the Mac detects the camera, it should automatically switch to Import. If it doesn't, click on "Import."

Importing from a Picture CD

1. Insert the CD into the Mac.

2. Open iPhoto by double-clicking on the icon.

3. Select "File," then "Import." Locate the CD in the Finder Viewer.

4. Select the images that need to be imported into the photo library. To select more than one image to be imported at a time, hold down the Shift key while clicking on the images,

Organizing Your Photo Library

Photo Rolls

iPhoto forces some kind of organization by storing the imported photos on rolls. To see your rolls, select the Photo Library. If you don't see the rolls associated with each import, select "View" from the top menu bar, then "Rolls." Now the images should be separated into their rolls.

Select the roll to give it a name that's useful to you. (The roll will turn blue.) The new roll title appears in the photo library.

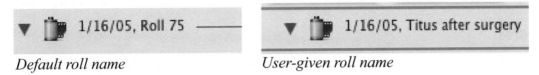

Default roll name   *User-given roll name*

Photo Albums

Pictures can also be organized into albums, just like the photo albums that you can buy in stores—except now you can create them digitally on your personal computer. This makes it easy to turn a photo collection into a story.

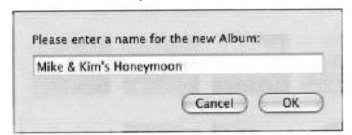

To create an album in iPhoto choose "New Album" from the "File" menu. A pop-up menu appears so you can name the album. Or you can create a new album by using the "Add Album" button.

The album now appears in the "Source" menu of the iPhoto software. Drag the pictures into it that you want included in the album one at a time, or select multiple photos and drag them in all at once. As the pictures are added to the album, iPhoto indicates how many pictures are included in the album.

It is now time to organize the new albums. In order to tell a story with the pictures you have to first put them in order. Select "Organize" and then drag and drop the pictures in the order that best tells your story.

Once the images are all placed in the right order, give them a title and add comments.

This is a great way for you to journal about the different photography techniques you used in each shot, as well as the compression and resolution file data. You may even include ideas you want to experiment with at a later date or on your next picture.

Note: If you don't see these options on your iPhoto screen, you might not be in "Organize" mode.

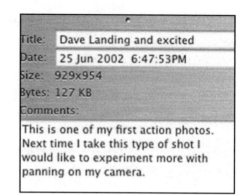

Photo Keywords

Another feature in iPhoto that helps you organize your photos is the ability to assign keywords to the pictures. "Keywords are labels useful for categorizing and locating all the photos of a given kind: vacation shots, baby pictures, mug shots, you name it" (Heid, 2003, p. 74). iPhoto even lets you assign multiple keywords to a single image. For example, if you have action shots from your vacation and your physical education class, you can categorize both images as "action shots" and then differentiate between the two by also categorizing one under "vacation" and the other under "physical education."

Keywords are a great way to quickly call up images in your iPhoto library. They sort through the images for you—no more searching in boxes and boxes of photo albums!

To assign keywords, double-click the key icon. You'll see iPhoto's predefined keywords. If these suit your needs, select the photo that you want associated with the keyword and drag the photo onto the keyword in the Keywords pane.

Editing Your Photos

Images in your album will probably benefit from a little bit of tweaking and editing. iPhoto's edit mode can fix many problems by resizing, cropping, enhancing images; eliminating "red eye"; and even adding special effects.

Select the image you want to edit and then select the "Editing" button on the iPhoto software. In the "Editing" menu, you'll have access to several tools (see toolbar on the next page).

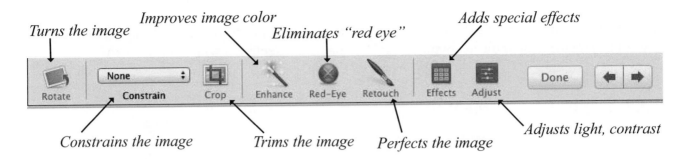

Turns the image

Improves image color

Eliminates "red eye"

Adds special effects

Constrains the image

Trims the image

Perfects the image

Adjusts light, contrast

Sharing Your Pictures

After you have put so much effort into shooting, organizing, and editing your images, you now want to share them with other viewers. iPhoto lets you share these images as a Web page, slide show, book, QuickTime movie, DVD, calendar, or blog. Use the icons on the "Organize" menu to access these options:

Printing Pictures

1. Select the images that you want printed.

2. From the "File" drop-down menu, select "Print." A pop-up menu appears.

3. Choose the preset option that best matches the type of paper you are using.

4. Under "Style Selection," choose the type of prints that you want.

Creating a Slide Show

1. Select the images that you want to include in the slide show.

2. Click on the Slideshow icon.

3. Use the Settings icon to select the transition type, the speed, and the length of time each image in the slide show will appear. Select your settings and then click "OK."

4. Click on the iTunes icon to select the type of music you want to play during the slide show.

5. The iTunes icon provides you with access to the songs you saved in your iTunes library. These songs can be included as background music in your iPhoto slide show. Select your song and click "OK."

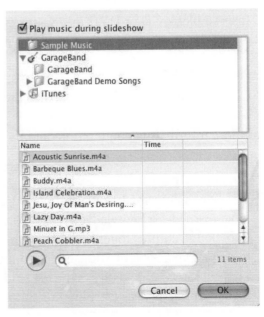

6. Click "Play" and your slide show will begin playing with the music you have chosen. (Note: If you want to stop the slide show at anytime, just click on the presentation with your mouse.)

Publishing Pictures on the Web

The Web is a great way to share your pictures with friends and family without sending big files through e-mail systems. iPhoto provides a quick and convenient way to create a Web site that can house your photos using Apple's .Mac service.

1. Select the album that you want to use to create your site.

2. Click on the iWeb icon.

3. Choose "Photo Page" or "Blog."

4. Choose a template for your Web site from the pop-up menu.

5. Drag and drop the pictures in an order that tells a story.

6. Make sure that you are connected to the Internet.

7. Click on "File" and "Publish" to your .Mac account. (Check "Send Me a Message" to allow viewers to send you a message.)

8. Once all the photos have been transferred, a dialogue box appears and displays the address of your new site's home page. Copy this address onto your clipboard and then send it to people so they can view the site.

Saving Pictures on CDs and DVDs

With iPhoto, you can save your photos permanently, on CDs and DVDs.

1. Select the album or individual photos that you want to burn onto your CD or DVD. To select more than one image, hold down the Shift key while you click on each image.

2. Insert a blank CD or DVD into your CD/DVD burner.

3. Choose "Share" from the top menu and select "Burn" from the drop-down menu.

4. Name your CD.

5. Click the Burn icon. iPhoto prepares the images and burns them onto the CD or DVD.

For more information about iPhoto and its other services, visit www.maclife.com/iPhoto.

Teacher Tips:
The books described on the following page are a great way to demonstrate what your students have learned—a knowledge entity—but they are also a great way to display all of your students' knowledge entities together in one portfolio at the end of the year. You may also want to consider making a yearbook of knowledge products—as a class—at the end of the year. This could display the best knowledge entity that each student created throughout the school year. (It would also be a nice addition to your teaching portfolio.)

Creating Hardbound Books

iPhoto can create hardbound linen-covered books from your digital photo album.

1. Select the album that you want to use to publish as a book.

2. Make sure the photos are in the order you want.

3. Click the "Book" button. You can now choose the theme for your book layout.

4. Select the theme of your book by clicking on the Themes icon on the bottom menu.

5. To edit the book, move from page to page by selecting the arrow buttons on the lower righthand corner.

6. Add photos to your book by dragging and dropping them from the top bar. You can include titles, comments, and page numbers. If you don't want to drag and drop individual photos, you can select "Autoflow" to lay out your book from start to finish.

7. When you are finished working on your book, click the "Buy Book" button.

8. If students are unable to purchase a book, they can either print out their books or save them as PDFs. To print out a book, click on "File" and "Print." To save a book in PDF format, follow the same instructions as to print, but select "Save as PDF format."

Assessing Student Progress

Your students are finally at the end of the Execution phase of their projects. It is now time to formally evaluate their performance. On page 161 is a rubric for you to use when assessing students who have chosen to be "Photographers" for their projects. Remember, it can be helpful for students to have this information at the beginning of the lesson so they know what is expected of them. For that reason, the rubric is provided as a separate page that you can easily copy and distribute.

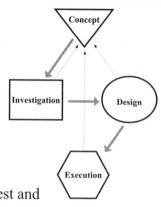

E-2 Tips for Better Digital Photography

Use the guidelines below to help you perfect your photography skills:

- **Get up close.** Get up close to show detail. If you can't get physically closer, use your camera's zoom feature. Really digest and understand the material.

- **Position the horizon.** In landscape shots, the position of the horizon influences the mood of the photo. To imply a vast, wide open space, put the horizon along the lower third of the frame and show a lot of sky. To imply a sense of closeness—or if the sky is a bland shade of gray—put the horizon along the upper third, showing little sky.

- **Kill your flash.** Existing light provides a much more flattering, natural-looking image, with none of the harshness of electronic flash.

- **Master your camera**. Many digital cameras have manual-exposure modes that enable you to specify shutter speed and aperture settings. Manually adjusting these settings gives you more control over tricky shots than automatic settings.

- **Crop carefully.** You can often use iPhoto's cropping tool to fix compostition problems. *But* be aware that cropping results in lost pixels, and that may affect your ability to produce high-quality images.

From Jim Heid's book *The Macintosh iLife* (2003).

Rubric: The Photographer

The following rubric will be used to evaluate your final project, your knowledge entity.

The library media specialist may be in charge of assessing this section of your project.

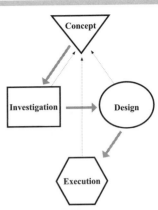

Phase	Not Yet	Okay	Excellent
Concept	The photographs are not indicative of the concept. It appears that little or no time was spent prewriting and analyzing the concept.	The photographs represent the concept, but it does not demonstrate that you came to a deeper understanding of the concept. It appears that minimal time was spent prewriting and analyzing the concept.	The photographs are indicative of the concept and clearly demonstrate that you came to a deeper understanding of the concept. It appears that a lot of time was spent prewriting and analyzing the concept.
Investigation *(see above)*	The photographs do not demonstrate results from your investigation. There is little or no information gathered. Information is not organized or authenticated.	The photographs demonstrate that you did minimal investigation. There is some information gathered. The information is organized but not authenticated.	The photographs demonstrate that you did extensive investigation. There is a lot of information gathered. The information is organized by virtual index cards, and all information was authenticated.
Design	The photographs do not follow your design. The photographs are not edited.	The photographs reflect your original design. The photographs are edited to help focus on the concept.	The photographs' execution caused your original design to change for the better. Photographs are carefully selected to share a moment in time or an emotion with the audience. The photographs are enhanced by editing.
Execution	The photographs show no creativity and are not fully executed. The photographs are not shared.	The photographs are fully executed. They represent the concept, but lack in true ingenuity. The photographs are shared.	The photographs show your unique talents and creativity: they could only have been created by you. You went beyond the scope of the book and found other tips to help you finesse your photographs. The photographs are shared in a manner that enhances the concept and leaves a lasting impression.

10. The Producer

Producers have software designed to help them edit, crop, store, and manipulate video footage to communicate an idea, sell a product, share news or information in a documentary, or share memories. iMovie is a great tool that will help you and your students share new insights learned about the curriculum and particularly the concept you are exploring. You and your students can start by shooting live video footage using a camcorder and then import the video footage, still images, and audio into a final project that communicates your students' new insights and understandings.

Movies can be quickly and easily created using iMovie and a video camcorder. Video footage is shot with the camcorder, which is then connected to the computer with a FireWire or USB port. iMovie, Windows Movie Maker or any other video software package you may use controls the importing process by storing video clips in a "clips" pane.

Video clips can then be edited and photos, transitions, titles, and effects can be added, by selecting the video clips and dragging them into a time line. Audio can also be added to the time line when students want to use music from their iTunes or songs stored on their hard drives. At the end of the process, the movies can be easily previewed with the "Play" button and then quickly burned onto a DVD.

> **Teacher Tip:** If you don't have any video editing software to use on your computer, but you have a camcorder and FireWire or USB cord, you might want to try www.download.com. There is a free-trial version of DVD Lab Pro 1.53, which is a nice video editing program. Or you might want to try out Power Director 4.0.

This chapter will help you and your students learn how to combine the skills you've learned regarding working with images and presentations, to create a fully produced movie. This will enable your students to show off their many talents in a new and creative way that will make a lasting impression.

Coming Up Next:
- Preparing a Movie with iMovie HD 6
- Sharing Your Movie

Execution

Preparing a Movie with iMovie HD 6

Follow the steps below to get started in iMovie on your Macintosh computer.

Not Sure of Your Software Version? To see what version of iMovie you are using, select the iMovie drop-down menu after the program opens and click on "About iMovie." A pop-up box showing the version number will appear. If you are using a different version of Microsoft iMovie and are having trouble transferring these directions to your version, visit this Web site: http://www.apple.com/support/imovie.

Importing Video into iMovie

1. Open iMovie by double-clicking on the icon, which is usually on the bottom menu bar on the Mac.

2. Connect the mini DVD camcorder via FireWire to the FireWire port located under the keyboard.

3. Turn the camera on and set the mode switch to "VCR" or "playback."

4. The Mac should detect the camcorder automatically; if it doesn't, switch the blue button to "camcorder."

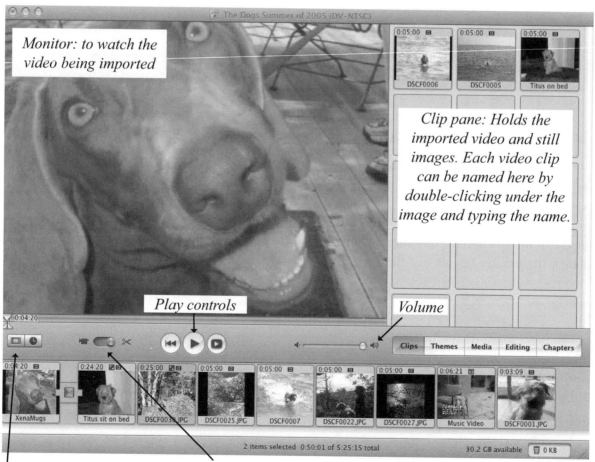

Monitor: to watch the video being imported

Clip pane: Holds the imported video and still images. Each video clip can be named here by double-clicking under the image and typing the name.

Play controls

Volume

Timeline/clip view button

Import/edit button: To import video footage, switch to the camcorder; to edit, switch to the scissors.

5. Use the "Play" and "Rewind" buttons to start viewing the video in the monitor. When you see some footage you would like included in the movie, select the "Import" button. As the video clips are imported into iMovie, they are displayed on the Clip Pane, where they can be labeled. *Note: iMovie automatically begins a new clip each time the camcorder is left on standby or is shut down, although you may still be importing the video footage.*

6. After all the video footage is imported to the video shelf, you can start sequencing the video clips on the video pane by dragging and dropping the video clips from the video shelf onto the video pane. Once the clips are added to the video pane, they can be rearranged by dragging and dropping them on the video pane.

Editing Your Video

It's important that your students focus their video footage on the main idea of the concept—and get rid of any extraneous junk. To eliminate irrelevant portions of video, use the crop feature of iMovie.

> *Caution:* If you are planning to add a transition to the clip, make sure it is longer than you would have normally planned.

1. Select the video footage that you want to crop, from the video pane or video shelf.

2. Click on the dashed ruler beneath the monitor and use the two cropping triangles to designate the video footage you want to keep.

Cropping triangles

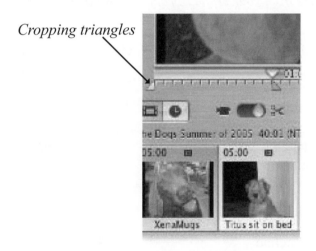

3. To crop out the remainder of the video, go to "Edit," then "Crop" at the top of the screen. Remember, if you don't like the crop, you can always select "Edit" and "Undo Crop."

Sometimes you may want to split a video clip into separate video clips. Having two video clips will provide you the freedom to edit each section of the video clip separately, instead of the clip as a whole. To split a clip, from the "Advanced" menu, select "Split Video Clip."

Adding Audio to Your Movie

The Clip View feature is great for viewing large thumbnail images of your video footage. It is also a good tool for working on the sequence of your video; however, it is not good for adding audio tracks to the movie. You need to use the Timeline View to add the audio, adjust its levels, and work it into the movie timing.

1. Switch from Clip View to Timeline View by selecting the clock icon.

2. Select the Audio pane from the icons available under the video clip shelf. You now have access to your iTunes.

3. Drag and drop the songs you want to include in your iMovie onto the tracks below the images during which you want them to play. There are two tracks where songs can be added to your movie. In order to turn off the volume on any of the tracks, use the check boxes at the end of each audio track.

Check boxes to turn on the audio track.

Drag and drop your songs from your iTune library or hard drive.

You can also record and add your own voice to the iMovie, in the Audio pane. Most Macintosh systems have an internal microphone to record your voice; if your system does not have an internal microphone, simply hook up a microphone to your computer and click on the record button to begin recording.

Drag and drop the play-head to make the sound file longer or shorter.

Editing the length of the sound in your iMovie is easy in the Timeline View. Select the playheads at the end of each sound file and drag them to extend the music or shorten them to shorten the length of time the music is played.

> **Teacher Tip:** If you are tech-savvy and have access to Garage Band, you can have your students create their own music. After they have created their own music, they can export the song to iTunes. After the song is exported into iTunes, it is made into an mp3 file and will be available to your students in iMovie.

List of special effects

Select the "Effects" button to see the special effects available to you.

Adding Special Effects

Special effects spice up any movie. They help engage the audience and enhance the producer's message. They can be used to make a film looked aged, to simulate a bright glare, or to apply a layer of "dust" over the video clips. There is even an "electricity" effect that adds a lightning bolt to the image or video clip.

When special effects are used sparingly and appropriately, they really add a "wow" effect to your production. On the other hand, when special effects are overused, they become distracting and take away from your intended message.

1. Choose the video clip or image that you want the special effect added to and have it displayed in the monitor screen.

2. Select the "Editing" button on the icons under the shelf and choose the special effect to be included in your movie under the Video FX icon.

3. After you have previewed a number of effects and are ready to add an effect to your movie, select the effect and click "Apply." The video clip will be rendered and the effect will be added to your movie.

167

Adding Transitions

Transitions are a great way to move from one video clip to the next and to help enhance the story. Certain transition effects are appropriate for certain circumstances. For example, a Cross Dissolve—the fading out from one subject to another—can be used throughout your movie whenever the subject is changing. On the other hand, a Fade In or Fade Out transition shows a lapse in time, while a Push transition is used to show a change in location.

Transitions are easily added to your movie using these simple steps:

1. Select the Transition button ![Trans] to get a list of transitions available to you in iMovie.

2. Preview the transitions in the monitor. Select the transition you want.

3. Click "Update" or drag the transition to the Viewer Pane. The transition is now part of the movie.

Transitions make add a really nice effect to your movie when they are used sparingly and consistently throughout the entire movie. For example, if you use the Cross Dissolve transition to change subjects in the first part of your movie, the Cross Dissolve transition should represent subject changes throughout your entire movie.

Adding Still Images to Your Movie

Photos from your iPhoto library can be incorporated into your movie quickly and easily. Photos are especially useful when creating documentaries. You can browse your iPhoto files in iMovie by selecting the Photos icon.

Select the album here that you want to view.

Browse your iPhoto albums here and choose the photo you want included in the movie.

iMovie includes a feature called the "Ken Burns effect." You can apply this effect to any of the images you want to include in your movie. What does the effect do? It pans over and zooms in on a still image, which can be useful in documentaries. Make sure the Kens Burn effect is not checked.

To add still images to your movie, follow these steps:

1. Click on the Photos icon to browse your iPhoto library.

2. Select the album you want to view using the drop-down menu.

3. Browse the iPhoto library for the image you want to include in your movie.

4. Select the image you want and then click "Show Photo Setting." The image is now imported into iMovie.

5. Click "Apply" in the Photo Setting Box, and the image is included on the Timeline/Clip View pane.

Adding Titles

Titles are an important addition to any movie. They are usually included in the opening scene of the movie to introduce a general theme to the audience. They are also included in the closing scenes as the credits scroll.

To add titles to your movie, follow these steps:

1. Click on the Editing button and then on Titles.

2. Carefully preview the different title styles available by clicking on them. There is even a style here for the end of your movies, called "Scrolling."

3. Decide on the font type, style, and color of the title. These buttons are located under the title transitions.

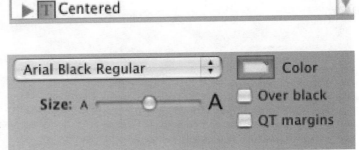

4. Drag and drop the appropriate title into your movie before the image where you want to title to display.

5. Add your title to the text box in the title pan.

6. Click "Add," and the image is included on the Timeline/Clip View pane.

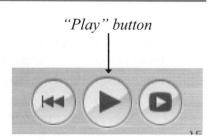

"Play" button

Sharing Your Movie

Now that you have finished creating your movie, what are you going to do with it? How are you going to show it? You can simply gather everyone around your iMac and play the movie using the "Play" button.

Exporting Back to a Tape

If you would prefer to show your movie on a videotape, you can export your movie back to the camcorder.

1. Insert a blank tape into your camcorder.

2. Reconnect the camcorder back to your computer with the FireWire.

3. Put the camera in "VCR" mode.

4. Choose "Share" then "Video Camera" from the "File" menu in your iMovie software. The "Export" dialogue box will appear.

5. Click on "Share iMovie." iMovie plays back your movie, sending its video and audio data over the FireWire cable to the camcorder.

Burning a DVD with iDVD 6

You have probably rented a DVD—so you know that at the beginning, it is broken up into sections and chapters. That is what iDVD lets you create. It lets you break up your movie into chapters. You can even burn your movie onto a DVD and play it on your DVD player at home!

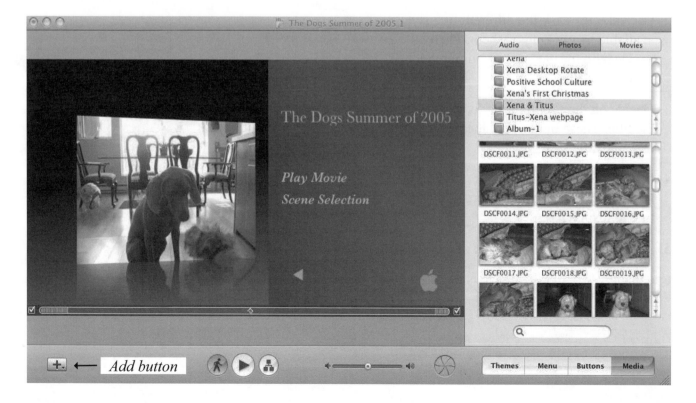

Add button

To create a DVD, follow these steps:

1. Select "Share" then "iDVD." Your movie is transferred to iDVD.

2. Choose the theme you want for your movie.

3. Click on the plus sign to add your movie.

4. Preview your movie by clicking on "Play Movie."

5. Use the Drop Zones to add pictures.

5. When you're done, click "File Burn DVD" to create your DVD.

   Note: Be patient. This takes a few minutes.

Themes

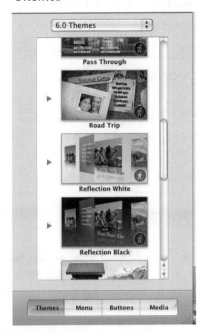

Now that your DVD is burned, pop it into a DVD player and share it with others!

Teacher Tips:

You might have each student in your class create a DVD at the end of the year as a digital portfolio of the knowledge entities they have created throughout the year.

It might also be neat to record each student in your room explaining their favorite knowledge entity and what insights it gave them into the curriculum. Then download this video footage and create a DVD to show their parents at the end of the school year.

Assessing Student Progress

Your students are finally at the end of the Execution phase of their projects. It is now time to formally evaluate their performance. On the next page is a rubric for you to use when assessing students who have chosen to be "Producers" for their projects.

Remember, it can be helpful for students to have this information at the beginning of the lesson so they know what is expected of them. For that reason, the rubric is provided as a separate page that you can easily copy and distribute.

Rubric: The Producer

The following rubric will be used to evaluate your final project, your knowledge entity.

The library media specialist may be in charge of assessing this section of your project.

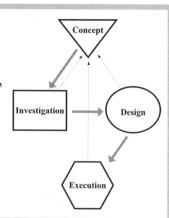

Phase	Not Yet	Okay	Excellent
Concept	The production is not indicative of the concept. It appears that little or no time was spent prewriting and analyzing the concept.	The production represents the concept, but it does not demonstrate that you came to a deeper understanding of the concept. It appears that minimal time was spent prewriting and analyzing the concept.	The production is indicative of the concept and clearly demonstrates that you came to a deeper understanding of the concept. It appears that a lot of time was spent prewriting and analyzing the concept.
Investigation *(see above)*	The production does not demonstrate results from your investigation. There is little or no information gathered. Information is not organized or authenticated.	The production demonstrates that you did minimal investigation. There is some information gathered. The information is organized but not authenticated.	The production demonstrates that you did extensive investigation. There is a lot of information gathered. The information is organized by virtual index cards, and all information was authenticated.
Design	The production does not follow your design. Your storyboard contains little information.	The production reflects your original design. Your production is storyboarded correctly.	The production's execution caused your original design to change for the better. Your production reflects the ideas in your storyboard, which contained the many details described in the blueprints.
Execution	The production shows no creativity and is not fully executed. The production type (i.e., fiction, documentary, or commercial) does not fit the concept.	The production is fully executed. It represents the concept, but lacks in true ingenuity. The production type (i.e., fiction, documentary, or commercial) suits the concept.	The production shows your unique talents and creativity: it could only have been created by you. You went beyond the scope of the book and found other tips to help you create your production. The production type (i.e., fiction, documentary, or commercial) enhances the concept.

Keane, *Internet-Based Student Research: Creating to Learn with a Step-by-Step Approach* © 2005.

Works Cited

Burmark, L. (2002). *Visual literacy: Learn to see, see to learn*. Alexandria, VA: Association for Supervision and Curriculum Development.

Dockterman, D. (1989). *Easy ways to make technology work for you* (4th ed.). New York: Scholastic Professional Books.

Heid, J. (2003). *The macintosh iLife*. Berkley, CA: Peachpit Press.

Index